ADVOCATING FOR MENTALLY ILL FAMILY MEMBERS

Janice Airhart

ADVOCATING FOR MENTALLY ILL FAMILY MEMBERS

Lessons for Mental Health Policymakers

Disability Studies

Collection Editor

Damian Mellifont

LP
Pp

Dedicated to family members who advocate for loved ones with serious mental illness. I am honored that they trusted me with their stories.

First published in 2025 by Lived Places Publishing

The author and editor have made every effort to ensure the accuracy of the information contained in this publication but assume no responsibility for any errors, inaccuracies, inconsistencies, or omissions. Likewise, every effort has been made to contact copyright holders. If any copyright material has been reproduced unwittingly and without permission, the publisher will gladly receive information enabling them to rectify any error or omission in subsequent editions.

British Library Cataloguing in Publication Data
A CIP record for this book is available from the British Library.

ISBN: 9781917566810 (pbk)
ISBN: 9781917566834 (ePDF)
ISBN: 9781917566827 (ePUB)

The right of Janice Airhart to be identified as the Author of this work has been asserted by them in accordance with the Copyright, Design and Patents Act 1988.

Cover design by Fiachra McCarthy
Book design by Rachel Trolove of Twin Trail Design
Typeset by Newgen Publishing, UK

Lived Places Publishing
P.O. Box 1845
47 Echo Avenue
Miller Place, NY 11764

www.livedplacespublishing.com

Abstract

This book includes firsthand stories from family members who have a loved one struggling with a serious mental illness. Each story was told in an interview with the author, describing the characteristics of the mental illness experienced by their relative and the effects of that illness on their loved one's ability to live a satisfying life and to maintain relationships. The intent of sharing these stories is to provide mental health policymakers with a deeper understanding of the effects of mental health policy and treatment practices on the family systems of those they serve. Recommendations for improved policy are provided.

Key words

Serious mental illness; psychosis; family involvement; mental health policy; HIPAA; involuntary hospitalization; advocacy; peer support; National Alliance on Mental Illness (NAMI)

Content warning

This book contains explicit references to, and descriptions of, situations which may cause distress, including:

- Suicidal thoughts, intentions, and actions
- Psychotic delusions and hallucinations
- Attempted violent assault

Please be aware that, due to the primary theme of serious mental illness, references to potentially distressing topics occur **frequently** and **throughout** the book.

Contents

Learning objectives

1. Define "serious mental illness" (SMI) and identify how it differs from a "mental health condition."

2. Describe the frustrations experienced by family members whose loved ones have a serious mental illness but refuse or struggle with psychiatric evaluation and treatment.

3. Identify how reading and understanding actual accounts of families who support family members with mental illness can be helpful for other families and for mental health practitioners.

4. Compare and contrast the benefits and drawbacks of HIPAA law as it applies to persons with serious mental illness.

5. Explore the value of involving family members in the treatment of patients or clients with serious mental illness.

1
Mental health stories matter

Introduction

Our individual stories matter, and our collective stories create a more complete picture of human experience. Some stories are harder to tell than others, however. One of the most difficult stories to disclose is one in which someone you love struggles with a mental illness. These are stories of loss and grief, but not in a traditional sense. The loss of an anticipated future with a loved one is like death, but it leads to a different kind of ongoing, recurrent grief that few people understand. Ongoing grief, in turn, can lead to silence and alienation.

Too often, those diagnosed with a mental health condition are feared or ostracized for behaviors that appear odd or simply different from others. Their behaviors can cause fractured relationships with family and friends. Sensational stories of violent acts by individuals who are deemed mentally unstable drive broader fears. However, according to an article in the Association of Health Care Journalists, those with a mental illness are more likely to be the victims of crime than the perpetrators of crime (Gray, 2022). Dispelling those fears requires understanding the dynamics of mental illness and its effects on both those who are diagnosed and those they are closest to. In addition, public policy should address the availability of mental health resources that will most effectively provide stability for families and their communities. While those who suffer from mental illness can and should make their voices heard to receive the care they need, family members have unique roles in supporting and advocating for each other. Depending on the affected individual's condition, the stories of those who love them may be the most relevant, reliable, or comprehensive accounts. In addition, stories of real people in real situations can have a greater impact than the presentation of academic principles.

This book includes lived experiences of **parents, children, siblings,** and **partners** of individuals diagnosed with a mental health condition. Some stories are complicated by multiple diagnoses, or by multiple individuals in a family who suffer from mental health conditions. Family members are inevitably affected by their loved one's condition, but in different ways, and some are left to shoulder sole caregiving responsibility. A sibling's obligation toward a sister or brother is quite different from a partner's obligation, however. This is why it's important to hear stories from multiple relationship categories.

Process

Interview subjects for this project were recruited through mental health agencies, personal or professional networks, or through online recruiting. Some participants were recommended by friends or acquaintances of the author. Others were invited to participate after sharing with the author personal experiences with family members diagnosed with a mental health condition.

Interviews were subsequently scheduled and conducted with individuals within the four relationship categories identified previously to bring to light the frustrations and successes experienced in caring for or supporting a loved one. While a consistent basic question framework was used to begin every interview (see Appendix I), each situation elicited additional questions to create a richer story. The goal was to identify useful resources or strategies that effectively control the negative effects of a loved one's illness. If efforts were made to advocate for them with mental health professionals or services, the results of those efforts are described. Brief descriptions of each of the mental health conditions mentioned in the book, along with hallmark symptoms appear in Appendix II.

In most stories, names have been changed to protect the privacy of the individuals interviewed and their families. Because some interview subjects previously published books about their family's encounters with mental illness, their real names are used. Each participant signed a "Consent to Participate in Interview Research" form prior to the interview, and each was allowed accommodation or accompaniment by another person of their choosing, if they requested it. Interviews were conducted in person when possible, or via Zoom online meeting, and often recorded to ensure accuracy in transcription. In whatever form they occurred, notes, transcriptions, and audio or video files are stored securely, accessible only by the author, and will be destroyed one year after the book's publication.

My story

My mother was diagnosed with schizophrenia in 1953 when I was an infant. Shortly after that, she was institutionalized in Mandeville, Louisiana, four hours from our family's home. I was ten months old. Aside from a few weekend home visits, my siblings and I did not see our mother for four years. Her hospital chart from that period, which I obtained in 2005, records visits by my father to see her, but none that included their three young children: my sister, my brother, and me. I have no recollection of her before 1957. Needless to say, I had no role in caregiving or monitoring her treatment.

In 1957, Mother was transferred to another facility in Pineville—Central Louisiana State Hospital—only two hours away. This meant the whole family could visit, but we only made the trek a few times a year. On these visits, we often took car rides into nearby Alexandria for ice cream. Mother generally sat, inert and quiet, in the front seat and interacted little with any of us kids in the back seat. I give my father credit for ensuring we made the trip so that we would see our mother, but I always wondered if she knew who I was. In the end, the bigger question for me became, "Who was my mother?"

When I was five years old, the year before I started first grade, Mother was considered stable and was discharged from Central State, provided she continued her regular Electroconvulsive Therapy (ECT) at a local hospital. I recall riding along to drop her off at the hospital and then visiting a local ice cream shop while we waited to pick her up. Ice cream obviously figured prominently in our visits with Mother. After each treatment, Mother was withdrawn and unusually quiet for a few days, though the calm never lasted long. While my memory is admittedly far from perfect, there are no memories of affectionate words or touch.

Meanwhile, I was fascinated by this woman called Mother and spent a good bit of time simply watching her. I imagine it was unnerving for her, but she never remarked on my tendency to lurk. While she was out of the hospital, my father took the opportunity to plan a trip from Louisiana to New Jersey to visit her parents, who cared for Mother's younger sister and her two children. My Aunt Mary had also been diagnosed with schizophrenia, but her parents chose to have her partially lobotomized. I don't know if she agreed to this surgery, and there was no one left to ask by the time I learned of it. In my grandparents' care, my aunt and her children were closely monitored and kept safe. It was the first of only two times I saw my grandparents.

My scant memories of Mother between June of 1958 and May of 1959 involve a lot of Coca Cola drinking and cigarette smoking. I often lay on the floor outside the bathroom and peered in fascination under the door to see what she was doing inside. Then there's a fuzzy memory of her making me open my mouth and stick out my tongue for her inspection. She was looking for evidence that we were being poisoned, and I dutifully complied. I don't remember thinking it odd at the time, which is intriguing in its own way.

Before my first grade year ended, things took an ugly turn. Her doctors evidently believed Mother could resume her role as mother and wife, as long as she continued her ECT and psychiatry visits in Lake Charles. They were wrong. The loud and angry arguments coming from my parents' bedroom at night frightened my siblings. Ever watchful, I must have been aware of the contention, but if so, I've forgotten it, along with most everything else.

Apparently, Mother was convinced Dad was trying to kill her. Maybe this is where I got the idea she thought we were being poisoned. She accused him of planting a spy in our home, as she was suspicious of the woman Dad hired to help her around the house during the days when he was at work. She complained she was being watched and that the housekeeper was thwarting her care of us. She lunged at him with a butcher knife once, as my brother recalls, but Dad was able to disarm her. I learned much of this later, after asking my siblings for their memories and after I'd obtained her hospital records, which included my father's account of their relatively short married life together.

The situation came to a head one day when my father was at work and my sister had a friend over to visit. Mother apparently went berserk over something my brother said or did and began hitting him and screeching in the front yard, a very public humiliation. My sister's friend ran home in a fright. Neighbors called my father at work and sheltered the three of us until he came home. Later, a police car arrived to escort Mother back to the hospital. She never came home again and died there eight years later.

Not only did my mother disappear from our presence, but it seemed my father erased her from our family. Though we continued to visit her a few times a year, he never mentioned her in between visits. I interpreted his silence as, "Don't talk about her. Pretend she doesn't exist." And so I did. As the silence grew, so did shame and guilt. No one else I knew had a family member who behaved the way my mother did. No one else's mother lived in a psychiatric hospital. Was there something wrong with our family? She'd been pregnant with me when her psychotic break occurred. Was I the cause of her illness? Would I also get the disease? I knew no one who could—or would—answer any of these questions.

After my mother's death in 1966, there was a certain amount of relief. My mother was dead; she no longer lived in a lunatic asylum, the insulting term everyone else used to refer to the hospital she lived in. Her death was more acceptable to divulge. I knew a couple of other kids at school whose mothers had died. Having a deceased mother elicited a measure of sympathy, which was a novelty. Disclosing that your mother lived in a psychiatric hospital got a very different reaction.

Not long after I turned 14, my father remarried a widow with three daughters, one of whom was a good friend of mine. My older sister married soon after, and my brother went away to college not long after that. I was left feeling alone and apart from this new family and the new school I was forced to transfer to. I no longer had a deep, dark secret about my family to hide, but I was thrown out of a familiar environment into a new home, a new school, and a completely new set of classmates. I kept mostly to myself.

Over the next four years, I felt like a fraud in my new family. My stepmother, whom I was delighted to call Mom, was not my "real" mother. My stepsisters were wonderful people, but we had different interests and different perspectives. Their mother was theirs, not mine—I didn't dare make too many presumptions. I married and left home less than a year after graduating from high school and moved on to a new life.

**

When I was 30 years old, the age my mother was when she was diagnosed with schizophrenia, I finally found the courage to ask my father a simple question: "What was my mother like? You never talked about her."

"I thought you weren't interested," he said, surprised.

I felt as though I'd been searching for the answer to this question all my life, and I found it hard to believe my father wouldn't have known it. By this time, I had two children of my own and sometimes struggled to mother my children without a role model. I'd had a caring stepmother, but we had different sensibilities, and I was mostly grown by the time she and my father married. I had no clue how to parent young people. Dad had also been a wonderful father in most ways, but I knew a mother's relationship with her children was quite different from a father's.

In answer to my question, Dad sputtered some basic information about my mother and listed some of her preferences. He told me how they'd met when he was in basic training in the Army during World War II and she was a young college student. They'd married as soon as he returned, wounded, from serving in Germany in 1946. In the next hour and a half, he told me more than I'd known all my life about a woman who had been little more than a stranger to me, yet he told me only disconnected facts. She liked playing card games and drinking daiquiris. She was a good student and typist. Her favorite color was blue. There were no fond stories.

And then he said nothing more about her. Ever. He died twelve years later.

I began investigating on my own in 2005 and felt extremely fortunate to obtain Mother's medical records from her first hospitalization at Southeastern Louisiana State Hospital. They are still the most concrete evidence of her existence that I have. Surprisingly, Central State, where she spent her final eight years, had no records aside from admission and discharge dates and a few demographic details. Mother's admission records in 1953 include my father's account of her first symptoms that led him to seek a judicial order for her commitment. He had told me none of this. When Mother was first admitted to the hospital, Dad reported several years of happy marriage prior to Mother's apparently abrupt change in behavior. However, the period just before and just after her hospitalization was the most painful of his life. He seemed caught off guard, unable to understand why she suddenly insisted neighbors were gossiping about her— neighbors whom he thought of as friends and who sometimes babysat at the last minute when needed. When Mother marched into her obstetrician's office in 1952, during her pregnancy with me, and demanded he declare his love for her, Dad became alarmed. She was referred to a local psychiatrist, with whom Dad seemed to disagree about her treatment, but with whom he eventually agreed that separation from the family was in everyone's best interest, for both Mother's safety and the safety of their three young children. He filed the papers to commit her to the hospital on the advice of her psychiatrist in 1953 and was left to parent us alone.

***

During my mother's first four years of residence in Southeastern State, treatment consisted mostly of Insulin Coma Therapy (ICT) and Electroconvulsive Therapy (ECT). The purpose of the first is self-explanatory. Her hospital notes documented how much insulin was administered and how many minutes of coma it resulted in.

From November 20, 1953:

> This patient started treatment on August 28, 1953. She finished on November 20. She had a total of sixty insulin treatments with fifty-one comas … She first went in to coma at 260 units, finished at 310 units. Her highest dose was 420. She showed some clinical improvement through therapy, was increasingly flat in disposition. However, her basic pathology did not change. The patient apparently had a secondary the night of October 12, or the morning of October 13. No other was reported. She, on occasion, went very deep but would lighten rapidly. She went very deep on September 16, had a very hyper-excitable period on November 6. The patient received 2,195 minutes of insulin coma or 36.58 hours.

Not long after this, my father requested the hospital discontinue ICT, although I don't know why. I've since learned that ICT, first used in the 1920s, was never an appropriate treatment for schizophrenia and fell out of favor in the 1960s.

However, ECT was and is still used for several mental health conditions as a "brain reset" of sorts. While primitive shock treatments are represented as barbaric in black-and-white movies and horror novels, current ECT procedures are safe and effective in treating certain cases. There are drawbacks, long-term memory retention being one. Over the four years Mother was a resident, her chart recorded ongoing and frequent accounts of her ECT treatments, accompanied by seizures and occasionally by injuries sustained from thrashing about or falling out of bed.

In addition to ICT and ECT therapies, my mother was often given barbiturates, codeine, or an anti-anxiety medication called Equanil, presumably to calm excitability or sometimes aggressive behavior. Ironically, she was also given anticonvulsive drugs to control the seizures brought on by the ECT. Since the effect of all three forms of treatment was to dull a patient's reactions and lead to coma or coma-like states, it's clear that the primary treatment objective at the time was simply controlling external behaviors. My mother was prone to delusions and persecutory thoughts, which would have been minimally affected by any of the treatments. In addition, the effects of any of these treatments long-term would have been damaging to her body. It is no wonder that she died "in her sleep of a heart attack" at age 42—or so we were told.

I have no records of her treatment beyond 1957, but I presume my mother benefited from some of the early antipsychotic medications like Thorazine or Haldol that were introduced in the 1950s and 1960s. If these were part of her regimen during the final years of her life, they apparently did little good. Her condition never improved enough for her to be released, and she died at Central Louisiana State Hospital in 1966.

***

The only time I visited Central State after my mother's death was in 2019, after the death of a sister-in-law who lived in Pineville, where the hospital was still located. It was no longer used for long-term residential treatment but housed a small clinic that included short-term hospitalization in one of the newer dormitories. The hospital was built in 1906 as the Louisiana Hospital for the Insane. Dozens of abandoned buildings and residence halls, in varying levels of disrepair, dotted the 409-acre campus in 2019, along with several brick buildings on the National Historic Register. The hospital, at its peak, housed more than 3,000 patients in the 1950s, around the time my mother lived there. It's now a ghost town and appears on several online lists of haunted sites. For me, the recent visit was both a homecoming of sorts and a reckoning with my past. I hadn't been there since 1965, when our family's church hosted a picnic in my mother's honor on the grassy-green rolling hills that make up the hospital grounds, sloping down to the historic dairy barn complex, once the site of positive employment for residents. These were the only features I recalled from my youth.

***

I've had decades to dream about what might have been possible for my mother, had she been born fifty years later than she was. Schizophrenia is not a "curable disease"—at least not yet—but many people, including at least one whose story is told in this book, find treatments that control their most troubling symptoms. Because many with diagnosed conditions lack the self-awareness or rationality to seek appropriate care and to conscientiously adhere to prescribed regimens, family members are their best allies in maintaining good mental health. For this reason, counselors, therapists, and physicians who treat the mentally ill should include family in any treatment plan. No patient or client can be treated in isolation.

Unfortunately, there were no services available to our family in my mother's lifetime, and my father did the best he could to cope with what few resources he had. It has only been in recent years that I've sought any support for my motherless childhood. Schizophrenia deprived me of the love and care a mother might have provided, but how could I know what I was missing? It's hard to grieve the loss of something you never had, but that was my dilemma. At the same time, I often chastised my adult self for not "getting over it."

Several years ago, I discovered the National Alliance on Mental Illness (NAMI) chapter near me and took a couple of their classes designed for family members. Unlike me, everyone else in the classes had a loved one they were currently caring for or advocating for. Over the course of several weeks, participants were educated about specific mental illnesses and treatments and provided resources to consult for accessing appropriate diagnosis or treatment help. Some of the stories I heard in those group sessions were heartbreaking. Many were frustrated by the lack of providers covered by their insurance or the lack of providers altogether in their community. Even when a provider was located, appointments could be months away. Some could not get a specific diagnosis for their loved one and therefore could not get appropriate treatment. Others found that because their family member had multiple diagnoses (not uncommon), treatments were very complicated. At each meeting, though, the sense of sharing frustrations with others who understood them was overwhelming. I kept thinking what a lifesaver this kind of community would have been to me in my teens, my thirties, or even my fifties. Instead, for years I dealt with my emotions mostly alone, while journaling.

Writing my full story, in the form of a memoir called *Mother of My Invention* was a great help in putting my childhood experiences in the context of decades of adult experiences, particularly those as a parent. I also consulted a therapist while writing it, and she helped me focus on painful incidents. At the same time, my editor kept advising me to "lean in" to the discomfort by writing more deeply about difficult situations. Reflecting on them from a more distant perspective took the sting out of them. I'm a firm believer in the value of writing to process emotions. For me, it's the best therapy. Others find relief in community.

Once my book was published, I held multiple book events where I could talk freely about the impacts of my mother's mental illness on me. Telling my story gave others permission to tell theirs. After each discussion, I'd hear from someone: "My aunt was in an institution, but my mother said never to talk about it," or "I just found out my grandmother suffered from mental illness. I wondered why I didn't really know anything about her, but my dad never talked about her." Hearing their stories led to my determination to give these family members a voice. One young woman had been treated for cutting and depression. After one of my talks, she approached me with tears in her eyes. "I'm worried about my mom," she said. "I know what I'm doing hurts her, but I can't seem to stop." This one broke my heart.

Those who struggle with mental health conditions also deal with persistent and pervasive stigma. Their family members feel it, too, as I did as a child. Reassurance that there is no one to blame for a mental illness is important. While we don't understand as much as we'd like about what causes a person's reasoning ability to malfunction, there are physical, genetic, and biochemical causes, just as with any illness. The fear of contagion and the notion that an individual's refusal to "act right" is to blame persist, however. Odd behaviors generate fear, and too often we blame others for our fear. The homeless man who pushes a shopping cart down Main Street stuffed with the entirety of his belongings is not to blame for his schizophrenia. He isn't to blame for the posttraumatic stress disorder (PTSD) he developed after serving in Afghanistan or Iraq any more than my mother was to blame for her disease. At least my mother wasn't homeless, even if the last place she called home was a psychiatric hospital in Pineville, Louisiana. When I drove through the campus in 2019, after an absence of more than five decades, I was ready to let my mother rest. The hospital grounds are deceptively serene, and I like to think she benefited from the peaceful wooded trails, nearby Lake Buhlow, and the tall canopy of pine trees that stand like caretakers around today's ramshackle buildings.

In 2024, all the services once housed at Central State were moved near another mental health facility in Pineville, which seems to benefit clients of both. About half of the acres it once occupied are being subdivided into tracts for single-family homes and townhomes, a couple of parks, and office spaces. The cemetery, where around 3,000 former patients are buried, and a few of the historic buildings will be preserved. It will no longer be a ghost town. I don't know how future residents will feel about the history of the land their new homes sit on, but I like to think a vibrant community will soon redeem the haunting memories of the tens of thousands of lost souls who once lived there.

2
Parent stories

Introduction

Every diagnosis of bipolar disorder, PTSD, or schizophrenia is unique. No mental illness follows the same progression as another's, as evidenced by the diverse stories included here. In addition, a study of 180,000 Danish psychiatric patients revealed that 47% of patients in the study received a different diagnosis within 10 years of their initial diagnosis, demonstrating the dynamic nature of mental disorders over a lifetime (Neuroscience News, 2022). Some individuals struggle with more severe symptoms and find treatment a greater challenge than others do. Some find that prescribed treatments control symptoms for a time and then, mysteriously, they don't anymore. These uncertainties pose a challenge for the diagnosed individual, their mental health practitioners, and their families.

Just as the course of disease can vary greatly from one individual to the next, each family is also unique. Demographics, location, economic situation, and other factors play a role in a family's ability to effectively support a loved one with a mental illness. In addition to these variables, the relationship one has with their loved one changes the dynamics as an advocate or caregiver.

A parent's role in caring for a child is quite different from a spouse's role in caring for their partner or the limited role a child often plays when dealing with an ill parent. Societal expectations for appropriate parenting prescribe to some degree what a healthy relationship and healthy family dynamic look like.

As Ann's story demonstrates, mothers sometimes feel a disproportionate degree of responsibility for their children's health and happiness. However, fathers and mothers both invest emotionally in their children's well-being. For Beth and Walter, heartbreak at their son's disappearance will likely never heal. And for Sarah and John, caring for a son who resents and defies their care—while they now care for the teenage grandson their son cannot adequately care for—ensures they will remain engaged in this contention as far into the future as they can imagine. Like most parents, those who tell their stories here persevere with stubborn hope, committed to their children's welfare despite the often devastating challenges mental health conditions pose.

Ann

I chatted with Ann Batchelder over Zoom from my desk at home as she waited at a hospital for her husband to receive a bone marrow transplant for blood cancer. She described the follow-up to his transplant, which entailed diligent care on her part to ensure he doesn't contract an infection from his environment—she's an impressively dedicated caregiver for her family. Since Ann has published a book (*Craving Spring*) about her journey as the mother of a daughter with clinical depression and accompanying addiction issues, she suggested I use her real name and that of her daughter. I began our chat by asking her to simply tell me about her daughter.

"Olivia's a wonderful kid. I could tell when she was in grade school that she was sensitive and learned differently from others. She doesn't pick up on social cues as others might." By the time Olivia reached puberty, though, things got trickier. Her peers picked on her, and they could be fierce. She was deeply unhappy. Ann and her husband moved their daughter to another middle school, but that didn't help. The situation was confusing.

"We have an older son who didn't have the same challenges Olivia did. We parented her the way we had parented him, but they just weren't the same." When Olivia was 15 and in high school, she was diagnosed with clinical depression and an eating disorder. She was prescribed medication for the depression and referred to a therapist who helped her work on her eating disorder. But soon she'd started to self-soothe with alcohol and eventually with drugs. "Although she had an eating disorder, the problem wasn't food," Ann says. Depression proved much harder to manage. Her coping strategies became physically harmful, but she couldn't process her emotions in healthy ways. "Her therapist told us, 'Most of us have a coating of Teflon that lets things slide off us, but Olivia doesn't have that.' I found that comment very helpful."

Ann says her daughter is creative, with big emotions that sometimes make her seem dramatic. "I was taught to tamp down emotions, and I didn't understand her heightened emotions were part of her personality. I kept trying to figure her out." Eventually Olivia got the eating disorder under control, but then there were a lot of stressful social changes in high school, like competing in debate class, playing hockey, or navigating friendships and boyfriend drama. In her senior year, she went through a breakup with her boyfriend and stopped trying to compete. According to Ann, once Olivia stopped trying to fit in, she found a group of peers at school that accepted and valued her. Unfortunately, these new friends had their own issues, including alcohol and drugs.

By the time Olivia was in college, she primarily coped with negative emotions by turning to alcohol and drugs. "She couldn't get a handle on them. And then she got arrested," Ann says. "At that point, she was assigned a counselor who was herself an ex-alcoholic, who didn't put up with bullshit." Olivia was required to attend Alcoholics Anonymous 90-in-90 (90 AA meetings in 90 days). Ann also began attending Al-Anon to process her feelings of guilt and shame. Olivia found AA meetings helpful, but in the end, they didn't address her fundamental issues. She signed herself into rehab when she was 20 and a junior in college.

"There's a misconception that you go to rehab and you're fixed in a month," Ann says. "But there are core issues that need to be addressed, and getting to them takes time. In counseling, they deal with issues in layers. For Olivia, it was understanding negative self-talk, self-esteem, and mindfulness." Five months after entering rehab, Olivia finally realized that controlling her depression would be a lifestyle and a mental health issue, not an issue with food, drugs, alcohol, or boys. She realized wellness depended on her own mental health, and this discovery was a game-changer. That didn't mean she was free of problems, however.

"Olivia was fine for a couple of years, with a few relapses, never as bad as before, but it's not a straight line. It's a lifelong process. If you take one crutch away, like the drugs or alcohol, you have to replace it with something healthier." Ann recommended some options to her daughter that she herself had found useful. Things like yoga, mindfulness training, and continued AA participation can all be healthy. "Going to therapy isn't enough, though. You also need ongoing peer support, someone to call in a crisis. AA provides a sponsor who is there for you anytime you need them."

Ann says the same kinds of support systems are helpful for the rest of the family as well. She has continued to attend Al-Anon and practices mindfulness exercises. Everyone in the family needs support in order for one member to get the care they need. It's the same whether it's mental illness or physical illness. For example, Ann's husband has blood cancer, and the Leukemia and Lymphoma Society has a program that helps families reach out to others who have gone through the same illness. "You're given the name of someone you can call at any time to ask a question or share a concern with. What worked, what didn't work. It's someone who has gone through the same thing." Ann believes this kind of support should be available to anyone with mental health issues, too. "Support groups are good but peer-to-peer support is best. Both the person with the illness and the caregivers need to be able to pick up the phone and say, 'I'm having a panic attack' and get talked down from that."

In 2016 Olivia chose to hike the Appalachian Trail, which was a healthy step in managing stress. "It was good therapy, but unfortunately, she contracted Lyme Disease on the hike. She now suffers from Chronic Lyme Disease." That has introduced severe complications in her healing process. It results in brain fog and body aches and exacerbates symptoms of depression. Making matters worse, she was undiagnosed for years. As mother and daughter are well aware, you can't treat a disease you don't know you have.

In spite of the challenges with her physical and mental health, Olivia got her degree and a certificate as a health and wellness coach. This was a positive step, "but she doesn't have the self-esteem to follow through with it," Ann says. She's getting better, but it's a lifelong struggle for Olivia and her parents. When things are going well, they're all tempted to think, "Okay, she's good now and we can relax. Now she's got her degree, now she's clean and sober, now she's got a purpose." Ann stresses that's not how things work. Things can change unexpectedly, which teaches everyone in the family not to take good times for granted. Timing that suits the family is not the recovery timing that works for Olivia. To cope with the ongoing nature of mental illness, it's important for caregivers to maintain compassion, empathy, and patience. As a mom, Ann wants healing to hurry up and relieve the pain of watching her daughter get better in fits and starts, but recovery is not a straight line.

In her role as mother, Ann ensures that Olivia—now 31—can access the resources she needs to stay healthy and tries not to obsess over what is out of their control. Ann finds solace in writing. "I need to see Olivia as empowered and not a victim. I also need a lot of support myself. Writing saved me." Writing helped her process what she and her daughter have been through together. Ann's memoir about their journey was published in 2023 (Batchelder, 2023). Publishing the book and talking about mental illness in a variety of venues and with multiple audiences afterward has brought a measure of peace and resolve. She learned there's no blame or shame in having a mental illness and wrote the book to demonstrate that others, especially family members, need not beat themselves up because of it. "You didn't cause it, but you need to be accountable for what your role is and how you walk that line. The book is how I walked that line." Writing doesn't have to be professional to be therapeutic, either, she says. Just seeing your thoughts on paper helps you ask yourself, "Is this true? How can I get help with this? You don't have to have professional writing experience to do this." Ann believes her story and others about mental illness help to dispel the shame that some families feel.

For centuries, there's been a pervasive societal attitude toward a mother's responsibility as the caretaker of her children's wellbeing. It ignores a child's innate personality and limitations, however. "It seems society believes that if there's a problem with a child, it must be the mother's fault," Ann says. "We do this to each other." When Ann realized the extent of Olivia's problems, she felt guilt. She was convinced she had done something wrong. As all moms do, she talked with friends about their relationships with their children, and it became clear that Ann's experiences were different from theirs. This hit home when she heard comments like these from other parents: "My kids are fine. At least they're not into drugs" or "At least they've never been in jail." Those comments were hurtful and made Ann less willing to share. She contends that judgments about how well a mother is doing her job are widespread even today and lead to shame when a child experiences problems.

The perception of a mother's culpability was epitomized in the "schizophrenogenic mother" theory by Frieda Fromm-Reichmann, popular in the mid-twentieth century, which blamed a mother's response to her children for causing schizophrenia (Hahn, 2020). Austrian psychologists Leo Kanner and Bruno Bettelheim piled on the guilt with the concept of "refrigerator mothers," who were deemed responsible for their children's autism, due to a cold disposition (Iannelli, 2024). Both theories have been widely discredited, but the subtle blame lingers, if only in the minds of mothers.

At some point, though, Ann stopped blaming and asked herself, "What can I do differently?" Instead of worrying that she was doing something "wrong," she began to disconnect from society's expectations and consider what she could do differently to help Olivia. Once she changed her perspective, she discovered there were many things she could do. She realized she needed to be honest about some of her own attitudes toward her friends' hurtful comments. "I needed to learn about compassion and accountability. I learned to listen better. I had to hear who Olivia was and not who I thought she should be."

Mothers of teens expect some resistance from their children, and it can be hard to separate typical teen behavior from unhealthy behaviors that signal a deeper issue. With a child who has a mental illness it's much harder to uncover the root of the behavior. "I felt out of control," Ann says. "It was harder because her illness led to addictions," and those addictions were more destructive than the illness by itself. Together, the illness and the frightening addictions made it difficult for Ann to understand the underlying issues and then recognize how she could respond.

Whenever Olivia experienced "addicted brain," Ann learned to engage in active support in new ways. It can take years to overcome the effects of addiction, and while Olivia healed, her mother stepped in to advocate for her. "Her brain chemistry can get messed up with drugs. I had to realize it was the illness speaking sometimes." That Olivia trusted her mother's guidance during those periods was a testament to the strength of their bond. Taking prescribed medication can be a challenge for many individuals who struggle with mental health conditions, but when there is a trusted support system, adherence to the regimen is more likely. Ann refers again to her husband's blood cancer and the necessity of taking medication on schedule. "It's similar with his cancer drugs, but the need for them is easier to understand," so he readily complies.

Changing her assumptions about motherhood was a turning point for Ann. "My mother assumed that if kids didn't turn out a certain way, it was the mother's fault, and she communicated that in subtle ways. Society thinks that, too, and it's not all that different from what my mother believed. Moms today are into blame and shame. There's still a lot of shame around mental illness and professionals don't give enough attention to changing that perception. It should be addressed at a professional level. In fact, they may unconsciously contribute to it." Consequently, Ann thinks this is where support systems and peers can be helpful. Eradicating the stigma surrounding mental illness requires more public discussion. Mental illness is an illness of the brain, just as a physical illness is of the body. It should be treated the same way as far as research and community networking go, but it's not.

For a physical illness, like a cancer diagnosis, "people bring casseroles or set up a CaringBridge account, but there's nothing like that when the illness is mental or your kid is in jail because they have a drug addiction." Family therapy is also offered for cancer patients, but it's not always available for families dealing with mental health issues. With family therapy, the goal is good communication between family members. That is especially important when an illness is as poorly understood as mental illness often is. When the disorder is mental, Ann says, "People distance themselves, because they fear mental illness is 'contagious.' Even parents isolate themselves and their ill child because they fear judgment. They hesitate to seek counseling and don't want to admit their child has a mental illness—it indicates failure on their part." Communication skills within the family have to be developed. "You've got to be heard and appreciated for who you are, and a lot of people with mental illness are reluctant to communicate when they feel there's something wrong with them."

According to Ann, there's value in reading about how other people have handled similar challenges. "When you're in the midst of a crisis, you don't know how things are going to go, but the stories help you see that there are lots of possibilities. A wide look is the best. What works for one may not work for another, or what worked once may not work again. It's good to see how others have coped, too." She thinks it would be helpful for mental health professionals to read widely about real people to help them treat patients or clients more effectively. It would be helpful if they could recommend books to patients or clients to help them feel less alone. Ann's husband enjoyed reading about other people with blood cancer and finding that while there were similarities, all stories are unique. It was helpful to find details he could relate to in many of them.

Ann says their family is much closer now than it was when Olivia was younger and no one understood why she was so miserable and disconnected. Mother and daughter have a better relationship. "It's much better than the relationship I had with my mother," Ann says. "My mother was okay, but I never felt I could turn to her for anything. I would never wish this on anyone, but it's been a blessing in many ways. It's a gift to have Olivia." Her daughter is stronger because of the challenges she's overcome. It's important for a therapist to not see Olivia as some "poor victim" now, she says. Her family is stronger, too, and that counts for a lot. "When our family gets on the same page, we can grow together moving forward and support each other."

The progress Olivia's family has made has taken time, though. Ann says it's taken 16 years to be comfortable with therapy that fits. It took trying different approaches to realize effective treatment needs to address the core issues and not only the symptoms. Olivia's current counselor, a social worker, is familiar with trauma therapy and spends time addressing belief systems. Over time, Olivia's worked with clinical therapists, addiction counselors, as well as a psychiatrist who prescribed medication for her depression.

Finding the right therapeutic fit isn't easy. "It's important to be flexible. You have to recognize when therapy is getting stale, too, and move on when you need to. Maybe a client has matured or a different issue needs to be addressed." Ann knows her daughter will always need support; finding what she needs when it's needed most will be an ongoing struggle. Staying alert to unexpected challenges and assessing what support is available requires frequently checking in with everyone involved. "Are things still working? Am I being honest with my therapist?" According to Ann, everyone in the family needs to ask these questions. A skilled therapist will likely detect when a client isn't being honest or completely forthcoming, but clients and their families are responsible for this self-analysis as well. Working together in family therapy is a good way to check in with each other occasionally. Understanding the specific family system is critical to effectively identifying the core issues for each family member, too. Not all families can afford the time or expense of trying out multiple therapists, and Ann realizes they are fortunate that they can pay for therapy out of pocket if necessary.

Olivia is doing well with external support and her family's encouragement. Recently, she and her mom took a beach trip. Both looked forward to some mother-daughter time together. Before they left, Olivia emailed Ann a list of six questions she wanted them to discuss on their trip. Ann doesn't know where Olivia found them, but all the questions were designed for mothers and daughters to grow closer. She was startled by this version of her daughter, who had the ability to surprise her in such a delightful way. "They were questions like: How do you want our adult relationship to move forward? What are you afraid of? Are there things in the past you still need to talk about?" Many mothers and daughters don't have such open and trusting relationships, and Ann is aware that what she and Olivia share has been hard won. "I was just blown away by her questions. I asked my husband, 'Who is this?' He said, 'She's your daughter, that's who she is.' He was right. She is my daughter, and she's an amazing person."

Beth

"He was driving from his home in central Texas to Colorado to bring his daughter a puppy," Beth says. "Felicia was 11 or 12 years old at the time and was living with her mother there. Jake stopped to visit some friends in the Texas Panhandle on his way up there. That's the last time anyone saw him. It was 2011, and Jake was 36 years old." Beth tells me they had suggested he have his female dog spayed, but he didn't listen, and unsurprisingly she had a litter of puppies. "He got it in his head to bring Felicia a puppy, and his dad and I asked if he'd told her he was coming, but he hadn't. We asked if he even knew her mom's address, but he didn't answer. He just went."

Neither Jake's body nor his truck was ever found, but he is presumed dead, Beth says. "The Texas Rangers found his gun at a pawn shop in Albuquerque a few days later, and there has never been another trace of him. It's still an open case, but it's now a cold one. They haven't gotten any leads in years."

***

Beth married Jake's dad, Walter, in 1980, when Jake was five years old. "Walter's wife had left him and their toddler son a couple of years before and didn't suggest taking Jake with her. I had two daughters from my previous marriage, one 10 years old and one an infant." Walter, Jake, Beth, and her two girls moved to a new home together. Beth empathized with Jake, because she believed he felt abandoned by his mother. His former family life wasn't dysfunctional and his parents hadn't been loudly contentious. They were both good people, Beth says, but she knows Jake struggled after the divorce. His mom remarried, and according to Beth, his stepdad was a mean alcoholic. She thinks it was probably best that he didn't live with them. She says he seemed constantly angry as a child and resentful of the baby. "I had to keep a close eye on her. I never saw him try to harm her, but I knew he held something against her. I never understood why. He just seemed to have a chip on his shoulder."

Blending two families with children can be difficult even in the best of situations, Beth says. It's disruptive to everyone. The first years weren't easy. "We worked hard on it, though. We even went to family therapy at one point—which no one besides me really wanted—but they went, and that helped." Beth spent much of her professional nursing career in psychiatric nursing and was familiar with mental health issues and the value of family counseling. Encouraging her new family to attend seemed a proactive step.

When Jake started school, he made friends and seemed to be happier. He had some special education needs, but he was intelligent enough and was doing okay, even if he wasn't all that interested in school. "When he was in fifth or sixth grade, the school had him tested and determined he had attention deficit hyperactivity disorder (ADHD). He was eventually prescribed Ritalin." Beth says they were grateful the school took the initiative to test Jake. "He didn't have a problem with hyperactivity and had never had behavior problems, but he had trouble focusing. He took Ritalin for several years, and it helped his concentration, but by the time he was in late middle school, he decided he didn't want to take it anymore." Around the same time, Beth arranged for Jake to see a psychologist for his anger issues and he went for a while, but soon decided to stop that, too.

Beth says Jake had some wonderful teachers and made friends that he kept for years, for which she's thankful. He kept many of those friends into adulthood. "He graduated from high school, but unfortunately, despite our efforts to intervene, he was practically illiterate," Beth says. "They kept moving him on to the next grade, even though he couldn't read well. It was really frustrating." Nevertheless, Jake began working as a teenager and always tried to have a job. He continued to live with Beth and his dad until his early twenties. "We had one hard and fast rule at our household. The kids were not to spend nights with boyfriends or girlfriends. When Jake got his girlfriend pregnant while he was still living with us, we told him it was time for him to move out. He didn't marry his girlfriend but continued to have a relationship with her and was delighted with his daughter Felicia, as were Walter and I. Her mother moved to Colorado, but she let Felicia stay with us or with her father from time to time."

When Jake moved out of his parents' home, he found a travel trailer down by a nearby lake and lived a chaotic life. "Once, after Walter visited him there, he told me the interior of the trailer— a dirty, jumbled mess—was an analogy for Jake's brain. It was clear he wasn't thinking rationally, but we couldn't get help for him—or he wouldn't agree to get help. One night, several years after he'd been on his own, he called us and said there were helicopters circling over his trailer spying on him. He was afraid of what they might do. These were classic signs of paranoid schizophrenia. Felicia, who was 10 at the time, was staying with him, and we were worried about what she was being exposed to. We decided it was best to remove Felicia from the situation and we had her come stay with us. We also called the county mental health department and asked them to intervene, but they couldn't get out right away. By the time a deputy checked on him, Jake had calmed down. He had a remarkable ability to act reasonably when he wasn't possessed with delusions." Jake continued to insist there was nothing wrong with him and refused to see a mental health professional.

Beth says she and Walter took turns sympathizing with Jake's impulsive and reckless behavior and administering tough love. They went back and forth, one of them sympathetic, the other stern. "It was stressful, but we were really scared he would kill someone on the road when he got drunk or under the influence, which happened way too often."

In the years after moving out of their home, Jake's mental health became more unstable over time. Beth or Walter often urged him to seek mental health care, but he refused. He would work for a while, get fired, and then find something else. Jobs never lasted very long. He wasn't financially responsible and often behaved recklessly. He didn't keep up with everyday details of life, like paying bills on time or filing and paying taxes. At the same time, "Jake tried to be a good dad to Felicia. He loved her, but his behavior could be erratic, and we worried it would put her at risk. He often had car accidents and DUI arrests. I think now some of these incidents may have stemmed from drug use, but I'm not sure. At one point, he was riding his motorcycle and ran off the road. Someone found him unconscious in a ditch with a deep gash in his head." Beth doesn't know why the person who found him called an ambulance instead of the police but thinks he would surely have been arrested again. It might have been another missed opportunity to get him mental health intervention. Instead, he was taken to the emergency room to have his wounds cared for and sent home. Beth and Walter suspect he had taken methamphetamines, but again, they had no way to be certain. At the least, he was acting maniacally and demonstrating symptoms that might have led to a mental illness diagnosis and treatment, beyond the ADHD.

After another incident in which Jake was arrested and in jail, "We begged law enforcement to have him evaluated for a mental health condition while he was there, but they wouldn't. Once he was released, there was no chance for it. That was in 2011, the year we last saw him." Beth says they still speculate on what happened to their son. He might have run into trouble and veered from his intended destination, or he might have been the victim of foul play. It's odd that his pawned gun was the only trace ever found of him. "How in the hell did anyone let him have a gun in the first place?" Beth wonders. "His dad and I were constantly terrified he would use it to commit suicide or to harm someone." She thinks it's possible someone murdered Jake, maybe for his truck or the gun, and then pawned the gun. Jake may well have been dead by the time the gun reached Albuquerque. After all this time, they're not expecting any answers.

***

After working in emergency room nursing for many years, Beth was employed at several different psychiatric facilities, many of them residential services for youth with mental health conditions. She found the work compelling and completed graduate courses for a master's degree in psychiatric nursing. As a member of the Air Force Reserve, she sometimes worked in the Lackland Air Force Base psychiatric unit as a psychiatric nurse. She also occasionally worked on projects with what was then the Texas Department of Mental Health and Mental Retardation (MHMR) and other governmental agencies in quality management before pursuing a PhD in nursing. MHMR was abolished in 2004. Around the same time, community mental health and state mental health services were reconfigured and responsibilities of MHMR were reassigned to other agencies. Much of the local mental health services provided in the Central Texas county where she lives became known as Integral Care.

Beth's education and work as a mental health professional inform her perspectives on appropriate care for individuals with mental health disorders. "In the 1970s, there was a push to move mental health services out of residential psychiatric hospitals and into community mental health programs, but they weren't strong enough to provide what patients needed. There just weren't enough community mental health resources, and the law didn't have sufficient criteria to allow families to get their loved ones the treatment they needed." She says the conditions haven't really improved since then. "Current laws are barriers to providing good care. It all comes down to the state legislature and what they're willing to pay for. It's simply not enough. Just finding a psychiatrist is a challenge. If you're lucky enough to find one, good luck getting an appointment within six months."

According to a 2024 article in *The Texas Tribune*, 246 of 254 Texas counties are designated "mental health professional shortage areas" by the federal government. The article also points out that not all people with mental health concerns require a psychiatrist. Other appropriate professionals include psychologists, social workers, licensed professional counselors, behavior analysts, and other therapists. Still, there are 5 million uninsured residents, many of whom depend on Medicaid for health care, and many available providers don't accept it (Simpson, 2024). To make matters worse, cuts are regularly announced for the inadequate community services that *are* provided. The Integral Care budget approved in 2023 for the following year would force steep lay-offs and elimination of programs, according to members of the United Workers of Integral Care union. (Aldridge, 2023).

"This is the direct result of legislators not prioritizing mental health needs," Beth says. "They pander to voters by cutting property taxes, but I would rather pay a little more in property taxes than cut mental health services." The problem seems to be growing, with evidence on many downtown streets across the US, according to Beth. "Just last weekend, Walter and I drove to the downtown train station to pick up a visiting friend, and because we were early, we waited for her in the car. Walter got out to stretch his legs, and a gentleman came up to him. At first, I didn't think anything of it, but soon the man was ranting loudly and yelling in an angry voice. I thought he'd started an argument with Walter and I was worried about a confrontation between them. Then I realized the man was verbalizing voices from inside his head and shouting irrational thoughts, which had nothing to do with Walter. He soon moved on. Because he was not presenting an imminent danger to himself or to Walter, there was nothing law enforcement could do. It was still disturbing."

In Beth's opinion, the criteria for intervention are too narrow. The man they encountered at the train station was innocent enough, and she certainly doesn't think he should have been arrested. But this was someone's brother or father. Did they know where he was? Were they worried about him? Would his family have wanted something done for him? "Street corners are full of people with mental illness," she says, "and I believe there are ethical issues with not taking action, if action might improve a family member's circumstances. What are the right criteria? The current ones may not be appropriate. Is it better to allow a human being to languish because of a mental illness, terrified of imagined foes, or is it better to impose treatment that would lead to a more satisfying life?" Beth says she doesn't know the answer. However, the criteria may be more a reflection of a lack of resources than what is in the best interest of the person, in her opinion. Beth cites the low number of state residential psychiatric hospitals as one critical service not available to many in a state as populous as Texas.

From a family member's perspective, Beth now knows what a lack of resources means when caring for adult children who won't care for themselves. Parents may be able to force evaluation and treatment for mental health conditions in their minor children, but with adult children, there are fewer options. "If there were adequate service options available—which there are not—we could present them, but many like Jake refuse to consider them." As a family, though, Beth believes she and Walter could have benefited from community organizations that educated them on what resources were available and facilitated access to them. She has greater knowledge about mental illness symptomatology than many family members might, and that knowledge is critical. Families need to understand symptoms and the possible progression of mental illnesses affecting their family. Being able to meet and discuss their struggles with other parents of children with mental illness is also helpful, but Beth was not aware of any such support groups during Jake's life.

Another important consideration for families is the safety of minor children in the care of a mentally ill parent. "Felicia's mother didn't really want her, and her father wasn't able to care for her adequately, and now he's dead. She spent some time with Walter and me, but her best support came from Jake's mother and his half-sisters, the daughters she had after marrying his stepfather. They all loved her and were good to her. They provided good examples of a functional family and gave her a stable home after Jake disappeared." Felicia lived with her aunts for several years, until her mother reappeared and asked her to come to Montana with her, where she planned to marry. "Every child dreams of being wanted by their mother, and Felicia was thrilled her mother asked her to come and be part of her wedding. She dropped everything and went. She was 15 or 16 at the time. It didn't work out, as I could have predicted, but she never really came back either. She visited a few times and would call us from time to time asking for money. We gave her some for a while but finally told her we couldn't do that anymore. We haven't heard from her since." Beth says she and Walter worry about her and wonder how she is. Even Jake's sisters don't hear from her. "I'm comforted to know that she did have some loving examples in her early life and hope those experiences will sustain her. We're still sad she chose to cut all of us out of her life." Beth shrugs. "She knows where we are if she wants to contact us. She would be welcome here."

As for Jake, Beth and Walter have long presumed he is dead. While coming to terms with that has been heartbreaking, they find some relief in knowing that he is no longer in danger of hurting himself, his daughter, or anyone else. "If he'd ended up in prison for harming someone, it might have been worse. The constant worry about Jake was hard on Walter. All those years we tried to get help for Jake and we just couldn't get him the help he needed. Walter has had heart problems in the past, and I'm convinced it's related to the stress of worrying about Jake. He's doing better now. We support each other as well as we can."

Beth says that Walter would never say this, but because she knows he might be thinking it, she recently told him, "I would rather see Jake dead than in prison in the shape he was in." Without the mental health care he needed, these were the only two options available to Jake. In the absence of a greater commitment by policymakers to making mental health resources accessible or revising intervention criteria, there are countless others like him.

Sarah and John

"Ryan was a sweet, creative child, with a strong connection to animals. He loved to play dress-up," his mother Sarah says, when I meet with her and her husband John on Zoom. She says it's difficult to explain Ryan's personality today, at age 40, because his psychosis has changed him so dramatically. However, she describes Ryan as kind and sensitive to other people's feelings as a young child. "Things changed when he was in fifth grade. His father and I went to a parent-teacher conference, and his teacher described him as the class clown. She suggested we consider medication for attention problems." Sarah says she and her first husband, Ryan's father, were offended by the suggestion, but then things got much worse when he was in seventh grade. "A couple of his teachers told us he was hanging out with some undesirable kids. One teacher suggested we keep him busy at home and so distracted that he wouldn't have time to spend with the kids who were a bad influence. That year was a disaster. He essentially quit school. We couldn't keep him in school." Sarah says he became defiant and unruly, getting into trouble with the police and once yelling "Fuck off!" at his principal. Sarah and Ryan's dad separated around this same time, and she says it was an emotionally difficult time for all of them.

"I was the rule-maker, essentially," Sarah says. "Ryan's dad and I would rotate playing 'good cop' and 'bad cop.'" Sarah was mostly the enforcer and Ryan's dad was more lenient. Ryan took advantage of that by going to his dad whenever his mom tried to impose rules. When Ryan began having trouble with drugs and alcohol, they asked the police for help, which did little good. Sarah says Ryan spiraled out of control. He was caught shoplifting and was habitually truant. "A county social worker saved his life. As Ryan got into more trouble, she suggested he was demonstrating more than adolescent behavior and recommended we have him evaluated for a mental illness. She helped me get him into an evaluation center, but we had to assign custody of Ryan to the state to get him into the center. He was there more than a year, while he was tested in every dimension possible: educationally, spiritually, and mentally. He was about 15 at the time, and the next two years were total chaos."

Around this time, Sarah married John, and he has been a support system for her in the years since. "Ryan left high school to enter the evaluation center and had not graduated. The county social worker helped him enroll in a program called Northwest Passage, a residential high school for troubled teens here in Wisconsin. They helped him get his GED certificate." Sarah describes it as a positive experience. Students were required to work out every day, and the school had a strict schedule he had to adhere to while there. At the end, staff also planned an intense, week-long canoe trip for students. "It was a highlight for Ryan, a real accomplishment. He still talks about it." Perhaps more important, Sarah believes, is that Ryan could not take drugs while he was a student there.

John says Northwest Passage was a good environment for Ryan because of their rigid control over his schedule. "The timing was right at the time for what he needed," he says.

While Ryan was at Northwest Passage, he saw a psychiatrist and was diagnosed for the first time, though Sarah can't recall what that first diagnosis was. He saw both a psychiatrist and psychologist but later was admitted to a psychiatric hospital for mental health issues, the first of several hospitalizations. "We had to file three-party petitions to be able to get Ryan the help he needed, probably three or four times along the way. It's all kind of muddled together in my memory," Sarah says. A three-party petition is a legal document used in Wisconsin that requires three persons to provide notarized statements about a person's behavior that might endanger themselves or others. The petition, if approved, allows the court to hospitalize the individual involuntarily for a specified time period. It may be used for those who have mental health conditions, drug or alcohol addiction, or in some cases, developmental disability.

***

Ryan had a son with his partner, a woman who also has a mental illness, according to Sarah. When Sarah's grandson Jason was about a year old, Sarah and John felt it best to bring him to live with them, and he's lived there ever since. Jason is now 17 and a junior in high school. Thanks to living with Sarah and John, Jason is shielded from some of his father's more bizarre behaviors.

"About six or seven years ago, Ryan went off his medication and just disappeared," Sarah says. "He had disability income—very little, but at least something—and he used it to travel all over the country. He took buses to Las Vegas, Los Angeles, Phoenix, and elsewhere. I would hear nothing from him for months at a time." Sarah and John were frantic, not knowing if he was dead or alive. "We called hospitals and morgues. At one point, we hired a private detective to find him. It was frustrating and financially difficult, but we kept at it. Apparently, disappearing like that isn't unusual for people with mental illness."

Ryan has been on medications for about 20 years now. His drug regimen has changed often but none of them have been effective. "He's very psychotic," Sarah says. "Today, his case worker sent a message to me that they were no longer going to prescribe Adderall, which is a surprise. He's got such addictive behavior and has abused methamphetamine."

John says he thinks it's a good sign that they don't think he needs Adderall anymore. "He's been on it too long," he says.

Sarah adds, "He's been off and on it for years, and it's been a horrible thing for him. He'll complain to a doctor—and he's seen many of them—and will say he needs something to help him focus. I don't think his records follow him, so they don't always know what treatments or medication he's had before, and they'll prescribe Adderall again. Then he gets addicted and begs to be off it a few weeks later." Since Sarah doesn't have access to Ryan's medical records, she doesn't know as much about his treatment as she would like. "It's terribly frustrating to not even know his psychiatrist's name. We can legally provide information to the doctor—if we know who his doctor is—but we aren't legally able to get anything back. We learned this through the National Alliance on Mental Illness (NAMI). So again, we could provide background information to his doctor, but we don't even know who we'd communicate with. Ryan's perception is so skewed about reality that he can be a danger to himself and to others, but we aren't allowed to get involved with his psychiatric care. No matter what his mental state is, he's in complete control of his own treatment. Unless we can say, 'he's going to kill me' or 'he's going to kill himself,' we're not allowed to intervene. It's frustrating."

Sarah believes that resources where they live in rural Wisconsin are terribly inadequate, but Ryan does at least have a case manager, whom he sees on a voluntary basis, and with whom he has worked for about a year and a half. "When he was picked up by the police in Phoenix, Ryan was psychotic. The officer found my number in Ryan's things and brought him for hospitalization after talking with me. Ryan spent almost a year in the hospital there before he was transferred back to Wisconsin, extremely ill. We did another three-party petition, and he was hospitalized here for a long time." Afterward, Ryan entered a halfway house for a year, but then he was released. "They just opened the door and he left. And the cycle repeats itself. This happens to too many people. Between the street, dying, or coming back into the halfway houses, they just don't get well," says Sarah.

Ryan has continued to work with his case manager voluntarily, but the case manager's caseload is too high, and he's pretty hands off with Ryan unless there's a crisis. Regardless, he can only do so much with what services are available. Currently, the case manager is helping Ryan complete an application for public housing. He thinks Ryan might qualify with the county for residential care. "Ryan has admitted that he probably needs to be in a facility with some services, because he can't take care of himself," John says. This demonstrates some degree of self-awareness, which is a problem for many who struggle with mental illness.

Sarah received another message recently that Ryan had been calling law enforcement personnel and churches, evidently prompted by auditory hallucinations, to make them aware of aliens and other terrorists that want to do harm. "He will say he works with the FBI or the CIA and has been in contact with aliens. He'll call the sheriff's department and say he just wants to give them this information. He's calling churches because he thinks he's a spiritual advisor. He's got a lot of mental things going on all at once."

Sarah says Minnesota seems to have better mental health resources than Wisconsin. They lived in St. Paul for a while, and she thinks cities have more services than rural areas in general. She also thinks Minnesota state resources are more abundant. She noticed in the past a lack of education among law enforcement officers in Wisconsin that wasn't helpful. "Once, when we called officers to assist in transporting Ryan to a psychiatric hospital, two young officers came. Ryan was off the wall, ranting and psychotic. The officers had an argument in our living room about who would drive him to the mental facility about two hours away. Neither of the young men felt safe with Ryan, because they didn't understand mental illness. They seem better educated today. Now when we call, a team comes, and you can tell they've been trained in talking him down and trying to reason with him, to deescalate things. That's hopeful."

NAMI has been a lifesaver, Sarah says. "I didn't even know what schizophrenia was when Ryan got ill. When I attended the first Family to Family class for family members of persons with mental illness, I just sobbed. I realized there were people going through the same thing. In time, I would co-teach the Family to Family class in our community. I did that for four years and found it helpful for me to provide that relief to other families. I also did a lot of reading on my own about psychoses."

Although Sarah is now well-educated about Ryan's mental illness and what treatments would be helpful, her ability to work with him is limited by HIPAA (Health Insurance Portability and Accountability Act) rules. They knew one of Ryan's early psychiatrists, but that relationship didn't last long, and now she and John don't really know any of the medical personnel he deals with. "It's impossible to help a person in any significant way without being integrated into their treatment," Sarah says. "It makes no sense to me that there's this roadblock for families who want to know what's wrong with their family member and want to help them. Maybe you can do some counseling together, but that won't happen if the person with the mental health condition won't agree to it."

Because Ryan resists the notion that he has an illness, when it's mentioned, he explodes. That means Sarah and John are prevented from helping him until things fall apart. "We're the only people there to pick up the pieces," she says. "My sister works in law enforcement, and I hear from her that the jail is full of people with mental illness. The system is broken." She often has to resort to filing a three-party petition to gain treatment for him, which Ryan resents even more.

Ryan's son Jason continues to live with Sarah and John, and he is aware of his father's condition. "They have a distant relationship. It saddens me, but Jason doesn't want his friends to see his father," Sarah says. "He doesn't want to hear the delusions and certainly doesn't want his friends to hear them. We have an apartment in our pool shed and we can sometimes hear Ryan just yelling at the voices from the house. It's not a good scene for Jason."

According to John, "When he's psychotic, his delusions convince him that he's under surveillance and his behavior is embarrassing to Jason. Ryan constantly reports to law enforcement that he is being watched. The idea of being watched sticks in his brain so much that it makes him psychotic, and he just can't deal with it."

Ryan has been living with his father, but his father has Parkinson's disease and has recently fallen. It's not a good situation for either of them, according to Sarah. It would also not be suitable for him to live with his son, his mother, and his stepfather, which is why they're helping him apply for public housing assistance.

Due to Ryan's erratic and sometimes psychotic behavior and his sense that his mother is putting restraints on him, his relationship with her is often strained. "He is beyond rude to his mother, despite what she does for him. It's really not fair, because she does everything she can to support him, emotionally and mechanically," John says. "He attacks constantly in a very vicious way, and it's so sad."

"I've been the person who has collected people together for the three-party petitions to get him hospitalized," Sarah adds, "so in that way, I'm the bad guy, but at the same time, I'm the one who steps up."

John sees himself as a buffer between Ryan and Sarah and thinks he can mitigate Ryan's hostility. "Just for the sake of staying in touch, I will be available to him and will take him to the grocery store or to the bank to cash checks. I'm taking his housing application in tomorrow to get him a place to live." In some ways, Ryan seems to prefer dealing with John; John has never been an initiator and signatory of a three-party petition.

"I've had to draw down an iron door emotionally just to survive," Sarah says, something which she regrets but finds necessary. "I'm immune to Ryan's anger, but it also prevents me from loving him fully. He will sometimes apologize to me or say he loves me, and sometimes he'll accept a hug. But I can't let that touch me emotionally. I can let it all in or keep it all out."

Ryan can sometimes blow up at John, too. "We had to just get him out of the house one day and he blew up at everybody. The attitude changes from day to day," John says.

Sarah and John are challenged by many of Ryan's personal habits. "His hygiene is horrible, and he's often unclean," Sarah says. "He looks, most of the time, like a wild man. This causes Jason a good bit of anxiety, too. Ryan's living space can be so bad, it would be condemned. He says he'll clean it, but he doesn't. It's deplorable beyond description."

Other challenges stem from Ryan's inability to recognize his effect on his family. "He comes by at all hours and is oblivious to what's going on here. We may be busy with commitments or taking care of household tasks. John might be grading papers, and Ryan will come over and begin ranting about surveillance, a book he's writing, or something else, none of which makes sense. Frankly, it gets boring to listen to him. We don't say it, but we want to." Sarah says she thinks Ryan can read body language and probably understands when they're trying to avoid interactions. "It's difficult, because we are his people. We are his only anchors to reality."

Both Sarah and John are active advocates for Ryan and for others who struggle with mental health conditions. Besides Sarah's teaching NAMI classes in the past, she also teaches high school. She talks openly with her students about having a son with schizophrenia, and because she suspects some of her students also have family members with mental illness, she lets them know she understands what that means. "I tell them I can listen if they need to talk about mental illness with me. I answer their questions as honestly as I can. I tell them how frustrating it is that Ryan has a brain disorder that's not easily treated as another kind of illness would be."

John also teaches, but at the college level. "I teach a class called 'Advocacy,' oddly enough. Today I had a class with presentations, two on autism and one on the role of special education programs in school. Teaching a class is secondary to the way I approach the topic of mental illness in general. I work with students who are going to be teachers, and that's a form of useful advocacy."When I ask about suggestions for students in mental health profession programs, he says, "I think it would be helpful for those students to have more training in early detection. Sometimes it takes too long to realize there's a problem, and the behavior is not just a personality characteristic. There's not much information about what to look for in young people." Distinguishing mental illness from the typically awkward struggle of teens toward independence can be hard, as Sarah and John learned from their experience with Ryan. John believes teachers can be instrumental in early intervention because they see a young person consistently and could observe when problems arise.

Sarah claims more resources need to be committed to brain research to help understand what causes dysfunction. Better understanding can lead to better care. Ryan has had many treatments, but none have been effective, which is disappointing. "I'm just so disillusioned, burned out, and angry. Medication hasn't worked for Ryan. It feels like there's no help available; it feels hopeless. This is a strong thing for a mother to say because I love Ryan so much," she says, "but I sometimes wish his life would end so that he would be at peace."

3
Child stories

Introduction

Children have a limited responsibility toward parents until they are themselves adults. They are completely dependent on parents to sustain them physically and emotionally. Parents with a mental illness may or may not be capable of providing what their children need. Children's dependence on their parents generally creates a deep and lasting bond, although this relationship naturally transforms as a child matures and becomes independent. Where parents may initially provide all their child's needs, a child may be required to supply a parent's needs later in life and often feels duty-bound to do so.

While children may have little influence over their parents' well-being, they are greatly impacted by their parents' mental and emotional stability—or instability. For children of mentally ill parents, the impact is influenced by the age in a child's life at which a parent's illness manifests, the severity of the symptoms, and the stage of child development in which the illness occurs. Family structures can be complicated, and each is unique, but children do not have the autonomy enjoyed by parents or partners in a relationship.

In the child stories that follow, it is apparent that children can be wounded by a parent's inability to parent responsibly, or conversely, a child can become an active participant in their parent's care when that parent is mentally ill. Sometimes a child fills both roles, but at different times. Amy's story demonstrates the effects of a parent with a mental health condition on her early development, then later in life, the effects of assuming caregiving responsibility for a parent and stepparent with mental illness. Kate became her mother's caregiver in substantial ways when she was an adolescent, charged with keeping her mother's environment calm and her routines structured. Margo and her brother suffered the effects of their mother's erratic behavior from early in their lives and developed mental health conditions of their own, perhaps as a direct response to their mother's condition. Their story is consistent with a large research study which concluded that there are elevated mental health risks in children of parents with a serious mental illness (Rasic, 2014). The stories in this section demonstrate the many ways in which children can be casualties of their parents' mental illness.

Amy

The image is burned in Amy's brain decades later, as though it happened yesterday. "I could show you almost the exact spot today … or within a hundred yards," Amy tells me. Her grandfather was driving her to her part-time job. "I was probably 17 or 18," she says. There was a dirty and ragged man hitchhiking along the highway.

"That's your dad," her grandfather said.

Amy strained to see the man she had only a vague memory of. She wouldn't have known him if her grandfather hadn't pointed him out. Her father was diagnosed with paranoid schizophrenia before Amy was five. She'd heard about her father's diagnosis, how he'd been violent and irresponsible. While she had hazy memories of her father trying to hurt her mother, she didn't believe the stories they told her. Not really.

"I was sure everyone had exaggerated his condition," she says. Instead, as an adolescent, she fostered a fantasized vision of him as stable and successful. Aside from a brief stay at a widow's colony nearby, Amy and her mother lived with her mother's parents in Oklahoma for most of her childhood, for their own protection. Her mother remarried when Amy was seven, but there was a lot of turmoil in the new household. "I thought people were lying to me about my dad and that he would somehow sweep in and rescue me from the chaos of my mother's household."

After her mother's remarriage, Amy still spent many weekends and school breaks at her grandparents' home, both as a child and as an adolescent. Despite the secret conviction that her father wasn't as sick as they'd told her, and that they'd one day be reunited, she appreciated the stability her grandparents provided. She knew they loved her. And yet …

Seeing her father on the highway that day was disturbing. "I could barely function. It took several days for me to return to baseline. It was just very disruptive." She kept her feelings to herself, though. No one ever suspected the fantasies she'd harbored or how devastating it was to have her hopes dashed.

"It's the only actual memory of my dad upright and awake, the only memory really, until I was 21, when I was asked to come to the hospital to see him, where he was in a drug-induced coma." While replacing some flooring in the garage apartment of a rent house his parents owned and where he'd been living, he started a fire. The adhesive he used was highly flammable, and he was smoking. Hospital staff didn't expect him to survive the serious burns he'd suffered, so Amy was called to see him before he died. Although he eventually recovered, he didn't awaken when Amy visited, and she never saw him again. He died 14 years later.

***

Amy's mother visited her husband's physicians at the state psychiatric hospital where he resided when Amy was still young. The doctors advised her to divorce her husband for the family's safety, because he would not recover. Amy's mother complied, although divorce violated her religious principles. Only the fact that the divorce was "doctor's orders" made it acceptable.

"I strongly believe the divorce was a positive step," Amy says now of her mother's decision. She realizes today how significant her grandparents' protection was and why they provided a home for her and her mother for several years. Amy says her mother had her own issues and couldn't provide the protection her young daughter needed without the support of her grandparents.

Amy's not certain if what follows is truly a memory or if she'd been told the story so many times that it now seems like a memory. The story goes that once her father came to her grandparents' home and stood on the porch with a gun, demanding to see Amy. "My grandfather had his own gun and made my father leave." On some level, she cherished the fact that her dad cared enough to want to see her. She had no other indication that he or his family remembered her.

"I really had no contact with my dad's side of the family. The only interactions I had with his parents were when I was 18 and then at 21. I didn't interact with them again until 2004, when my father died. I was 35."

The unexpected gift she received after her dad's death was that his older brother David came into her life. "David became a keystone feature in my life, and we were very close until his death in 2017." Amy says her uncle taught her a great deal about the disease of schizophrenia. He had a substance use disorder and became a drug and alcohol abuse counselor. His mother, Amy's grandmother, was once interviewed for a newspaper article about the National Alliance on Mental Illness (NAMI). Her paternal grandmother was deeply dedicated to her son (Amy's dad) and active in NAMI's mission, doing the best she could for him with the resources available, which were few at the time. Amy's maternal grandmother saw the newspaper article and saved it for Amy. She didn't see it until much later.

When her dad had recovered from the burn episode and Amy still never heard from him, "I assumed he'd forgotten about me." She didn't even recognize how devastating that belief was until her uncle called to tell her about her father's death. As they grew closer, David began to tell her about her father, including assurances that he had not forgotten her. When they went to a doctor's appointment shortly before his death and a woman came into the room, her dad remarked, "that woman right there is about Amy's age, isn't she?" When David told her about the incident, Amy recognized that knowledge as a blessing. "Just to know he hadn't forgotten me was so powerful."

After her dad's death, Amy received a box of papers, including letters he'd written to his mother. In his letters home, her father alternately said he didn't want to ever see his family again and then a few weeks later he begged them to visit. Amy describes the perspective in his letters as "infantile," due to his illness. In a forensic assessment while he was in prison for auto theft, the record documents that he had spent most of the previous several years at the psychiatric hospital but had been discharged.

After release, he wandered over several states, getting arrested in both Arizona and Missouri before being sent back to the state hospital. He was prescribed the antipsychotic drug Prolixin, but it apparently didn't help much. In a letter to his mother when Amy was 20 years old, her father pleaded with his mother for help in getting back home and help in finding a more effective treatment. His plea must have been successful, because he ended up in a burn unit near his family home a year later.

"I knew I couldn't know him directly, but I have archaeological records in a way," Amy says. The box of documents is evidence of his existence and she treasures it. Ever since, she has wanted to learn about the disease he struggled with. Several years ago, she discovered a NOVA special on PBS that explained the unique MRIs of individuals with schizophrenia, and she absorbed it all. That was just the beginning of her education about schizophrenia. "I wanted to learn everything I could about it. There's always more to learn."

Amy at least knew a few inconsequential details about her father. Her mother told her that he loved Janis Joplin and John Steinbeck. "I walked to the public library and checked out every Steinbeck book. I still keep a Janis Joplin tune on my phone. Everyone talked about his intelligence and said he was book smart. He liked quirky things, when no one else in my life did." Amy believes she inherited her father's intellect, but the connection made her wonder if she would also get sick. The NOVA special reassured her that she was unlikely to develop schizophrenia because of her age and gender, but she has children and grandchildren. She worries for them, because of the clear genetic links.

As an adolescent, Amy didn't talk with others about her father. It was a family secret that she felt she needed to keep. None of her peers, aside from the father of her children, knew about her father's condition. She thinks the secret held the family together. A stigma persists to this day in disclosing mental illness that makes it difficult to talk about. "There's a public perception that if people would just act better, their symptoms would get better," she says.

It wasn't until several years ago at a local training session for emergency responders that Amy felt comfortable sharing her story. She now meets many people with stories of their own and has since become involved with NAMI after her Uncle David's death in 2017. She shares her story in 40-hour Crisis Intervention Training (CIT) sessions for her local police department, fire department, and other local public service agencies. In her presentations, Amy emphasizes three points: the public's negative reaction to chronic mental illness leads to shame and isolation, safety when an individual is in crisis is a significant concern for both the individual and the responder; and the need for professionals to demonstrate compassion toward those who are mentally ill.

***

It would seem traumatic enough for any one person to have lived experience with only one family member with a serious mental illness, but Amy has direct experience with two. After divorcing Amy's dad, her mother remarried a man she'd only known for a few weeks. Amy was 7 and lived with her mother, her stepfather, and two younger brothers until she was 16. During those years, her stepfather had substance abuse and drunk driving issues. He could become violent as well. Amy describes a lot of his behavior as manic; he worked as many as three jobs sometimes. His behavior created a chaotic household. Years later, he was diagnosed with schizoaffective disorder, a condition that presents symptoms of both schizophrenia and a mood disorder, such as bipolar disorder.

"My stepfather is a high-functioning schizophrenic," says Amy, which probably explains why he wasn't diagnosed until much later in life than is generally the case. Most men present symptoms in their late teens or early twenties.

Her mother and stepfather are still living independently, though her mother is now suffering from cognitive decline. Amy responds when her stepfather contacts her, but she doesn't often initiate communication. He cares for her mother as he is able, but Amy worries that he may be abusive. However, the couple appear satisfied with their situation. "The abuse dynamic is still there but the severity has declined," Amy says. Despite numerous pleas from her three children, her mother refuses to leave him. At least her stepfather adheres to his medication regimen, demonstrating some self-awareness. "I respect him to some degree for that." Amy and her brothers work together to provide for their parents' basic needs. "Groceries, rides to doctor's appointments, whatever they need."

***

When asked about the resources she and her family have relied on, Amy mentions the unequivocal support of her grandparents. "My dad was clearly a formative figure in my life, and my stepfather has been influential in shaping my view of the world, but my grandfather has been the archetypal father figure in most ways."

Outside the family, Amy cites the resource that would have been most helpful to her and her siblings: education. After the chance encounter with her father on the highway when she was in high school, she was devastated. She knows it affected her behavior. She had some interaction with a school guidance counselor, but the counselor knew nothing about mental illness and couldn't have been much help. "The guidance counselor at school would know something was up and would call me in. But she didn't have the knowledge—it wasn't available. The experiences were emotive but not constructive." There are more resources available today and school counselors are better able to assist students who experience substance abuse disorder in their families. This is helpful, but not necessarily related to mental health. "Better education can go a long way to reducing stigma and shame." Some families might also need economic support or intervention. But education is key, Amy insists. Supportive peers and mental health professionals are essential resources.

Amy doesn't believe her mother would have accepted support, but she and her brothers have found NAMI classes and support groups helpful. "My mother doesn't have an active diagnosis, but that she married two men with mental health conditions is mind-boggling. She clearly has issues. I love my mother, but she doesn't know how to keep people safe." She and her brothers have developed empathy and compassion, Amy says, but they didn't learn it from their mother.

At this point, Amy's stepdad appears to take pride in being a caretaker for his wife. That he is high functioning helps. He hasn't worked since 1992, and that's been hard for him to accept. Remaining active keeps him engaged. He is an extrovert and enjoys social interaction, but Amy's mom does not. He's established a daily routine for the two of them that suits him, one that involves a visit to McDonald's and a day center for seniors. "Mom would never have agreed to this before, but she doesn't fight it now."

The mental health challenges Amy and her brothers deal with in their parents are both acute and chronic. They keep a running document in a shared folder so they can track what's happening. She thinks of herself as an advocate for people with mental health issues, even among friends and the students she now teaches in college biology courses. She sometimes hears complaints about the accommodations offered to students or a student complaint that they can't do something, and she finds herself advocating for those with limitations, while still challenging them to perform. "I am much more aware of people's neurocognitive limitations. The limitations are real," she says, even for her and her brothers. They don't trust their own memories or perceptions completely, which is why they keep a shared document going. It helps create a more complete picture when they all contribute their observations. "I feel very lucky to have my brothers to share the responsibility."

Having a cell phone to record photos or videos is also a recent but valuable resource to help keep everyone accountable. Amy's parents aren't reliable narrators, so unbiased recordings are useful. The record sometimes speaks for itself.

Another resource that Amy believes has been immensely helpful is the psychiatrist who works with her stepdad to get the most effective treatment he can. He was struggling with sleep issues, and his psychiatrist began increasing the dosage of Triazolam, to the point that some pharmacists refused to fill the prescription. "She stuck with it, though," Amy says. "She kept working on it until she found a pharmacist who would, and it's made a huge difference in my stepdad's ability to sleep." It might seem a small thing, but good sleep supports all the other treatment efforts.

In addition, the doctor ordered genetic testing, which revealed a vitamin B metabolic problem. From there, additional components were added to his regimen. Things have been much more stable since then. Not every psychiatrist would have gone the extra mile this way, according to Amy, but they've been working together for a decade or more. Her role as an advocate for her patient has been so valuable to the family.

"We go to his appointments with him," Amy says. "His doctor sees and hears us." She understands how important their support is and works with them to resolve issues.

Amy's brother is currently serving on their local NAMI board of directors, a post that Amy recently vacated. "It's related to his

work with mental health crises," she says. And while NAMI's educational resources are excellent, Amy wishes they would evolve
more quickly to accept recent discoveries and treatments related
to schizophrenia. There is resistance from some in the organization to accept the genetic components of the disease, and she
believes there should be space for more conversations about
genetic risks. Amy is concerned for her brothers and her children and grandchildren. "My stepdad's genes are a part of my
brothers' gene structure. My father's genetic makeup is carried
over in mine. I can see some of those genes in my grandkids." The
genes carry both risks and benefits, of course, but "limiting risk
for first-episode psychosis in vulnerable populations is helpful."
Early detection and treatment are advantageous, but intervention prior to the first episode would be even better.

"Science makes gains faster than the average person can keep
up with. NAMI is slow in adopting some of those things that
come up in pop culture. Aside from epigenetic changes to DNA
caused by trauma, there are legitimate gene clusters related to
impulsivity, which are factors in substance abuse disorder. The
gene cluster won't disappear, because those with the impulsive
gene cluster are the most likely to reproduce. We literally know
the gene cluster, but culture doesn't keep up with the science.
The bigger the organization, the slower the change. Not a bad
thing, but there's a need to catch up."

Amy feels she's in a better place today, secure in good friendships with colleagues and others educated about mental illness.
"I don't have to worry that disclosing my history will put my job
at risk, as it might have done 40 years ago." At the same time, her
experiences have made her determined to be a good advocate

for her family members, those who are ill and those who aren't. She's discovered strength in her ability to transform the shame or anxiety she once felt surrounding those in her family who haven't always acted in her best interest. "I'll never be powerless to them again. When you don't have your own vehicle, your own space and music, and your own friends, or good coping strategies, you're at their mercy. Being trapped with that madness makes you vulnerable."

Social services can help release children from these circumstances, if they provide adequate education about mental illness to school counselors and others who work with children, Amy says. Guidance counselors can be a first line of defense. Training fire and police about mental health crises is also helpful in deescalating situations. Having embedded support in first responders is vital.

The most important concept to embrace in improving the situation for families in crisis is wraparound services, Amy insists. When social service agencies and law enforcement and healthcare professionals communicate with each other, for example, better support of a family will result. "We need people who will check in with a family to see how they're doing. It's expensive, and maybe not always easy to find people to do it, but the effort can save lives." Amy cites the national 988 Crisis Hotline initiative as one example of a service that attempts to offer wraparound service by coordinating communication between agencies. Their city has had a groundbreaking crisis hotline like this one for more than twenty years. They have evidence that a wraparound strategy works. It's not uniformly administered in other places, however. "In the last calendar year, children have lost their lives because they didn't have wraparound support and a seriously mentally ill parent. We won't catch every case, but that's where I think we can make the most difference." Following up on families after initial contact or intervention can be complicated when they are unhoused or mobile and can't be located, but Amy feels it's important to try, because it's the best way to build bridges to safety or life-saving resources.

None of these public services can compare to the support and encouragement loving relationships can provide, however. Knowing you can count on family or friends to be there for you is crucial. Amy credits her grandparents and her brothers for fulfilling those caring roles in her life.

"My brothers are the greatest gift my mom ever gave to me."

Kate

"In many ways, my childhood was the exact opposite of yours," Kate tells me when we meet over Zoom. She had read my memoir and knew my story describing our family's experience with schizophrenia. Despite her mother's schizophrenia diagnosis, Kate had the benefit of her mother's presence in their family's life. Kate says her first 13 years were fairly normal, as her mother managed to function to some degree throughout her life. My own first 13 years were anything but normal and concluded with my mother's death that year. Kate's mother died in 2015 at age 83, after having lived in an assisted living facility for several years, along with Kate's dad. "Mom never accepted her diagnosis, so we had to slip her medication into her drinks and such, but our doing so helped keep her symptoms manageable. We did this for decades, because she refused to take them if she knew what they were," Kate says. "It wasn't a problem in assisted living because the nurse would come and give Mom her pills, then give Dad his pills. Somehow she never questioned what kind of pills she was receiving there."

According to Kate, her mother's psychotic break happened in dramatic fashion and signaled to Kate that things would never be the same again. "My parents had a traditional marriage. Mom had been a small-town beauty queen, was beloved by her community, and held only one job, writing for the *Grand Rapids Herald Review* newspaper. A traditional homemaker and mother, she was a Cub Scout leader and Sunday School teacher. Dad, on the other hand, traveled extensively and often, all over the world." In 1966, when Kate was 13, everything changed.

"Mom woke my sister and brother and me very early one morning and urged us to get up and get dressed. 'We have to leave here right away,' she said. She told us that our neighbor, Gertrude, whom we knew well and loved, was going to kill my sister if we didn't leave immediately. She said we should get on our boat—we had a small sailboat—and sail to Pinole, across the San Francisco Bay." Kate knew it was not true that their neighbor had threatened her sister. While her mother was occupied with waking and dressing her siblings, Kate went down the hall to a phone extension and called her uncle, her father's brother. She told him what was happening and asked him to come. He lived about 40 minutes away at the time. "When I told him what Mom had said, he didn't ask questions. He just came. By the time he got to our house, Mom had calmed down a little and seemed to think it was a good idea for Uncle Frank to take us to his house for the day. She assumed we would be safe there." It was a school day, Kate says, but they spent the entire day at her uncle's house just visiting with him and their aunt. Nothing was ever said in Kate's hearing about her mother's previous panic over what she believed was a threat by their neighbor. "Mom took a long nap on the couch, and the three of us kids just played and hung out. Uncle Frank called my dad, who flew in and came to get us."

While it was clear to Kate that something was seriously wrong after this incident, her dad did not see things that way. "It took Dad a couple of years or more to finally admit that Mom was ill. Surprisingly, my little sister, who was 6 years old at the time, says she wasn't aware of anything out of the ordinary. She says she didn't realize Mom was sick until she was 15 or 16." While Kate is amazed that her sister was unaware of her mother's condition for so long, it likely is a result of Kate's and her dad's ability to control the home environment and to buffer the consequences of her mom's condition for Kate's siblings. "My brother understood that something was wrong, but his response was to absent himself. He was always gone. He'd get on his bike and go visit friends. He just didn't spend much time at home." Kate, on the other hand, was told that it was important for her to help keep her mother calm, and she did the best she could, despite her young age.

"It's astonishing to me today to realize that Dad didn't much alter his work habits and that he trusted me to keep things under control while he was gone. He worked in international mining and would travel all over the world to set up mines or to monitor their operations. He'd fly to Brazil or Japan to open a new mine and be gone for days or a week at a time." Kate says they managed while he was gone, her mom carrying on with her usual household chores as well as she could, and with Kate keeping her focused. Kate helped with tasks like cooking and taking care of her siblings.

"He wasn't willing to admit there was a mental illness right away, but Dad took Mom to her doctor, who prescribed Valium. She could get kind of loopy when taking it. Nevertheless, she drove us to school and other activities all the time. We must have had guardian angels because nothing bad ever happened. When I think about it today, I don't know how she managed to drive us all over town while taking that drug."

Once Kate's mom was diagnosed with paranoid schizophrenia a few years later, she was prescribed Haldol, which she was given surreptitiously because she refused to take it otherwise. Then she was prescribed a newer drug called Clozapine in the 1970s, which she took for many years, "I'm not sure what she transitioned to in her later years, but she took antipsychotic drugs all the rest of her life—without her knowledge. One of the early drugs caused her to have tremors later in life, though."

One of the strategies Kate's father instituted was to keep the home environment calm. "He let me know I was responsible to keep everything as calm as possible. 'Don't upset your mom,' he'd say. At the same time, he encouraged Mom to continue with her daily responsibilities like cooking, cleaning, and ferrying us to activities. He actually told her what he expected her to do, and she complied. It was important to maintain a routine, and because it was a routine Mom was accustomed to, it kept her focused and stable."

Kate's father had one inviolable rule, however. "Dad made it clear that he had zero tolerance for violence, and Mom seemed to understand it. She was by nature a gentle person, so it wasn't often a problem." She recalls only two or three times her mother was hospitalized, and each one was initiated by some violent behavior she doesn't recall. Despite Kate's attempts to control their environment, her mom's behaviors could still sometimes be erratic and she still sometimes expressed paranoia about someone she suspected of threatening her family with harm. "She once insisted we sell our piano because someone was going to kill our grandfather. We didn't do it, and she soon forgot about whatever threat she imagined. She was often afraid of terrorists, for some reason. There were several similar incidents, and we managed to calm her down and the paranoid delusion would subside. She could interact normally a good bit of the time." Kate says she's not sure if her mother experienced hallucinations, but she was often convinced of some threat of harm to herself or others. "She also sometimes had delusions of grandeur. For instance, she thought she was the true queen of England for a while. At one point she believed Dad was the president and that my brother was the vice president. We didn't contradict her, and eventually she would forget about her delusion." Kate describes another incident that landed her mother in a local police station because of her innate generosity. "Mom's niece was graduating from veterinary school and Mom thought it would be nice for her to own a pet store. Consequently, Mom had written a one-million dollar check to purchase a store for her. Clearly, there wasn't that much money in their account." Kate also says her mom had an imaginary nemesis named Ivy who would play tricks on her at times. According to

Kate, most incidents were related to her fear of a random person threatening someone she loved.

Kate's paternal grandfather had died in middle age, and her father and his siblings, although young, had taken care of their mom from that point on. Kate believes this is why her dad felt it was appropriate to give her so much responsibility for taking care of her mother. Despite Kate's taking on a decidedly adult role in managing her mother's behavior early in life, especially while her father was traveling, she isn't bitter or resentful. She accepted her role willingly because, in her mind, she was maintaining peace at home. However, she says one reason she kept an optimistic attitude was because she had a wonderful support group in the form of girlfriends from school. They bonded over a variety of problems with their mothers. "One had an alcoholic mother. One girl's mother had divorced and remarried. Her step-dad would chase her around the house when her mother wasn't home—she spent a lot of time at other people's houses. Another mom had breast cancer, and one was just a bitch. We supported each other. I would relate what my mother had done, and we would all have a good laugh over her crazy behavior. It was a great outlet and helped me face our situation with a measure of good humor. I never felt a stigma around mental illness with these friends."

However, Kate believes the strong stigma regarding mental illness was what kept her mother from accepting her diagnosis. "She was unable to see herself as mentally ill because of the very negative attitudes toward mental health conditions at the time. It was unfortunate." Her father was also aware of the stigma and didn't expose his wife to his business colleagues for that reason, although they attended church together. Kate describes one unpleasant experience when a pastor suggested that her mother was the victim of demonic possession. He barred her from teaching Sunday School, something she'd done in the past. Her behavior could be disruptive and confusing, but the pastor's remarks were upsetting. On a positive note, Kate says she's read that children of parents who are mentally ill often enter health or creative careers. "This has played out in our family. My sister was an emergency room nurse most of her career, and I am an artist, painting mostly portraits."

While Kate accepted her role in keeping things calm around the house, it wasn't without anxiety. At the end of a school day, when Kate arrived home, she didn't know what she would encounter. "It sounds odd, but as soon as I opened the door, I could 'smell' whether Mom had had a good day or not. If she had been particularly sick or frightened over something, there was a certain smell that permeated the house. Most of the time it was fine, thank goodness."

One of the coping mechanisms Kate's mom employed was something she referred to as her "supreme court work." She read the newspaper out loud to herself, cover to cover, every day. "She would take copious notes as she read—page after page of them. When she was finished she would write out a supposed court case to settle some event she'd read about. It literally kept her busy for hours each day. I think it kept her paranoia and her fear at bay." Kate described her mother's thought processes as very disordered sometimes, and Kate had to help her to complete her daily work, like the cooking and tending to the house. "It felt like

I was doing her job, but as I grew older, I matured and passed her up, while she never really did mature. Most people become wiser as they age, but Mom couldn't process events well enough to do that. Her illness prevented her from becoming wiser as she aged. How could she process a bunch of false memories and paranoid thoughts? It was impossible to synthesize them in a normal way." In the end, Kate says her dad was very proud of her mom's ability to cope as well as she did. He outlived her by several years and often told Kate and her siblings that he was taking good care of himself so they wouldn't have to take care of their mom. "And he did. He was 93 when he died, several years after Mom passed. Because his father had both a heart attack and a stroke before his death at a relatively young age, Dad was determined to overcome his genetics."

***

Kate says their family had no support system to help them during her mother's life. Her mother's sisters were distant. "They'd send birthday cards, but they never called." They thought her mom disturbed their parents too much and tried to keep them apart. As a result, there wasn't much interaction with her maternal grandparents. "Mom had no friends. Her only close friend stopped calling or spending time with Mom after her illness became pronounced. It would have been nice for Mom to have some social connections. I'm sure she was lonely. She could have used someone to talk to besides her family." According to Kate, this is where community mental health services might have been beneficial. Having someone conduct home visits, even for short check-ins would have been helpful, she says, even if only to ensure the children weren't being harmed or being expected to do too much. "A social worker checking in on us occasionally would have been good."

Kate has lived in Texas for many years now, while her parents stayed in California, where she grew up. She or her parents visited back and forth between the two states as often as they could over the years, but it wasn't the same as living nearby. "They came to visit us in Texas whenever they could. Sometimes Dad would leave Mom here if he had to travel for an extended period on business. He would bring her medication in liquid form and leave it for me to administer." That could be tricky, Kate says, because then they had to make sure her mom drank all the juice or soft drink the medication was mixed in or that Kate's children didn't accidentally drink it. "It could be quite nerve-wracking sometimes, almost comical." She was glad she could give her dad some relief on those occasions.

Kate's younger sister and her parents bought a house together at one point, when their parents' age became a concern. Her sister had been a nurse and took wonderful care of them. "She and Dad bickered a lot, so it wasn't ideal for that reason. He wasn't used to having anyone question his decisions, and my sister didn't take any crap off of anyone," Kate says with a laugh. Still, she gives credit to her sister for taking excellent care of their parents while the three of them shared a home, before their mom and dad were moved to an assisted living facility and sold the house.

While Kate says she hasn't gone out of her way to advocate for individuals with mental health conditions, her father was active in National Alliance on Mental Illness (NAMI) programs during his life. Kate and her husband currently volunteer with a program near their home called The Nest, for high school students at risk of failure in school. "We host a party for them every month to celebrate their successes. The program gives the kids a sense of community," she says, reminded of her group of close girlfriends in high school. "That kind of connection is vital for kids. I was so lucky to have had my group of girlfriends when I was in school."

All in all, Kate feels very fortunate for several reasons. First, her mom's illness didn't manifest itself until Kate was an adolescent. She has good memories from before her mother's symptoms began, and her mother already had ingrained adult habits that helped her maintain a structured life. Second, her father was the kind of person he was. He never complained about her mother's condition, and he coped with it in the best way possible during the 45 years of her illness. Finally, Kate is grateful that her mother's nature was inherently gentle. She very rarely exhibited aggression or meanness. While she says they sometimes had to reframe her mom's actions, they were never truly destructive. These elements of good fortune may explain why Kate's family thrived, while preserving good relationships. "We maintained a positive spin on Mom's actions for the most part, except when we had the rare visitors to our home. That could sometimes be embarrassing."

Kate's daughter said to her grandfather once, "Granddad, I'm so sorry you had to care for Grandma for so long when she was ill. It must have been so hard."

"Oh, honey," he replied, "she would have done the same for me."

"More than anything, this describes my father's personality," Kate says. "In spite of everything, they had a strong marriage. They had a sense of commitment to each other that helped him care for her all those years."

Margo

"My mom is the seventh of eight children in a somewhat wild and bohemian South African family," Margo says. "It's a big Catholic family. My grandparents were very devout and my mom and her siblings were steeped in that faith tradition—a very ethical family. They have a deep commitment to each other and to making the world a better place." Margo describes her mother as an activist deeply driven by principles of anti-racism and anti-apartheid. "That has always framed our family's life. It was the tradition in which my younger brother and I were raised." Margo's mom and several of her mom's siblings are employed in HIV prevention work. "They are driven to making the world as equitable as possible." Their convictions run deep and have been passed on to Margo and her brother.

When Margo was quite young, her mom was diagnosed with bipolar disorder. "She didn't accept the diagnosis, though. She rejected it and the medication they prescribed. She has a very complicated relationship with her condition; she defiantly flushed her lithium down the toilet for years. In the last couple of years, though, Mom has accepted some help. She now takes an antidepressant and meets with a therapist. She insists the medication is not for bipolar disorder, though." In addition to prescription medicine, Margo says her mother self-medicates with marijuana, which is legal in South Africa. While she used to drink heavily, she no longer does, contributing to her more stable condition today.

Margo fully accepts her mother's bipolar disorder diagnosis. "I know other people who live with manic depression, what bipolar disorder was once called, so it's easy to see these symptoms in my mother. It aligns perfectly with her actions. As far back as I can remember, her behavior has been erratic. One day she was Super Mom, up at 6 a.m. to make homemade lunches for my brother and me, heating our clothes on cold mornings before we put them on, all maniacally so. On other days, she was totally depressed and exhibited distress or anger." Margo says her mother loves music, and married Margo's father because he was a musician. Her mom is also very artistic. "Mom was a painter for a long time."

A couple of years ago, after Margo moved to the UK, her mom went into a clinic for her drinking and hasn't had alcohol since. "The combination of no alcohol, mild antidepressants, and age, I think, in addition to a few other coping strategies, seems to have helped immensely." Margo visits her mother and brother in South Africa about once a year. Her parents are now divorced. She also has a half-sister, with whom she is not close.

Margo's mother engaged in anti-racism activism for a long time. Until recent cuts in foreign aid by the Trump administration, she worked for an organization that delivered care to HIV-positive mothers. "As of today, she's entrenched," Margo says. "She worked for them for a very long time. Many of our family members have been involved in that kind of work."

Margo is employed by a program called Changing Futures, a government-funded agency operated by the local council to benefit people who are *multiply disadvantaged*. "This is government jargon," she says, "which just means we interact with individuals with more than one challenge, such as: homelessness, substance abuse, domestic abuse, interaction with the criminal justice system, or mental health challenges. A person with more than one of these challenges is *multiply disadvantaged.* We don't deliver services but work to change systems." Changing Futures works in partnership with 15 communities across the UK and offers training and conducts research on ways to make systems more equitable. "I'm involved in inclusion and anti-racism allyship work."

While Margo's mother and her family of origin instilled in their offspring deeply ethical views of social justice, Margo was also exposed to a great deal of trauma because of her mother's bipolar disorder. "I've been diagnosed with complex posttraumatic stress disorder (C-PTSD)," Margo says. C-PTSD can develop because of prolonged or repeated trauma, with or without a history of abuse or neglect. "My childhood environment was unstable, where you never knew what you were going to get. I now know from my own research and from research in trauma informed practice that children need stability. I needed to know that when I got home, I could expect certain things. It wasn't like that at all. It was erratic, sometimes wonderful. Mom could sometimes be excited, ecstatic for us to go out for a lavish dinner, when we couldn't afford it. I knew we couldn't even afford to buy groceries." Margo explains that her world, her home, wasn't safe. Nothing could be taken for granted. "This instability contributed to my parents' divorce when I was 9. It created a very difficult environment to grow up in. My safety was wrapped up in Mom's safety, and Mom was not safe." As a result, Margo says she became hyperconscious of her mother's moods, how she was doing on a given day, and how she was managing her moods—whether with alcohol or other unhealthy behaviors. "It became harder and harder to separate her feelings from mine."

Margo's brother lived with their mother and sister after their parents' divorce as well and still lives with their mother. He has been diagnosed with clinical depression. Both children have responded to their mother's condition with mental health issues of their own. It may not be completely fair to assume their conditions are a result of their mother's behavior, however. "It's hard to pinpoint a cause, because there may be a genetic predisposition, but my brother's illness may follow the same trajectory as mine, which also evolved from depression. Our mental health conditions may be a function of our brain chemistry or it may be the way our brains have been trained through the context of our experiences and environments."

Unlike her mother, Margo has been diligent in seeking treatment for her C-PTSD. "I've had therapy since age 7. In 2016, when I was 24, I was hospitalized for two weeks for psychiatric assessment. I now have a psychiatrist, a psychologist, and am on medication. I've also had Eye Movement Desensitization and Reprocessing (EMDR), which tracks eye movements and helps reprocess memories." EMDR helps people heal from traumatic events by having them attend to traumatic memories in brief sequential doses while focusing on an external stimulus (EMDR Institute, 2025). According to Margo, EMDR therapy activates both sides of her brain when processing memories and allows 'refiling' in more appropriate places. It results in less triggering of unpleasant emotions and prevents the memories from retraumatizing. She says it keeps her brain online and encourages proper filing of memories.

One of the most supportive resources is one that Margo found through her job at Changing Futures and has found useful. It is called the Trauma Informed Plymouth Network (TIPN), a group committed to trauma-informed therapy. These techniques recognize the impact of trauma on individuals and design therapies with those specific traumas in mind. Practitioners first elicit the traumas a person has encountered, whether the result of a single event or ongoing sustained situations, as the root causes of their mental health difficulties. After establishing a trustworthy and safe environment, practitioners empower patients to participate in their own care by making informed choices about the nature of their therapy (Yadav, McNamara and Gunturu, 2024)

Margo is now a project officer with TIPN. "It has been gratifying to find a community of people who take my experience seriously and validate it. I just stumbled onto it in the course of the work I do with Changing Futures. I'd done some reading and was familiar with some of the experts and key thinkers in the field but wasn't aware of the network. That has become a critical resource." Changing Futures provides some funding for TIPN. Margo describes this work as advocacy. "I'm a mental health advocate in the sense that I research how we can improve people's lives, get them what they need. Our organization treats them as human beings who have had difficult experiences, without over pathologizing them or framing them as deficient. They're just living with difficulties. In a sense, I'm a professional advocate." In addition to her day job at Changing Futures, Margo is a poet and writer. She has published a book of poetry and recently submitted a book manuscript for publication in 2025.

Medical and psychiatric services in South Africa and the UK are similar in that both provide national health care, but, according to Margo, neither provides adequately for mental health. "The National Health Service (NHS) has failed in that regard. They're trying, but they're underfunded and over capacity. It almost killed me. The negligence of some practitioners when I first attempted to get help was extraordinary. I tried that route initially, but it didn't work. I pay privately for care now. It's what I need."

Margo says she now sees a general practitioner in the NHS, but she sees a psychiatrist who is paid privately. "If my psychiatrist changes my medication, my general practitioner prescribes it. It was too difficult to use the NHS for mental health care. The waitlist for a specialist is quite long. It took 8 months to see a psychiatrist when I got to the UK, even though I needed immediate help. I saw her once, then never again. Even with medical care, it appears getting adequate attention is 'the luck of the draw.' If you get a good general practitioner, which I have now, you are lucky. But this is the third one I've seen. The first one put me on a high dose of diazepam, which is highly addictive. The second one told me to get off of it, but cold turkey. It turns out that's dangerous. It left me with serious suicidal ideation, a common side effect of withdrawal." Margo is satisfied with her current physician, whom she describes as, "the first sensible person who is working with me to monitor and manage my medication dosages. There's a burgeoning mental health crisis in the UK. People are struggling and we are living in difficult and uncertain times."

Margo's mom has been able to utilize the National Health Service in South Africa to the limited degree she seeks it, but she only maintains a relationship with a therapist. Margo says her mother rejects not only her diagnosis, but much of the support that would be helpful. She has minimal interaction with her family of origin but a strong community of friends—a geographical community, according to Margo. "She knows everyone, and there's a cannabis lounge nearby where she knows many people and with whom she has good relationships. It's an informal kind of support."

Margo's brother has been in therapy in South Africa since his childhood and is on the same medication that Margo takes, which she finds interesting. His depression is well-managed at the moment so that he can work. Margo's husband, though, is struggling to manage clinical depression. "It has been acute for the past year. He is seeking work at the moment, and his depression has made it worse. He's not feeling very valuable or useful right now. Those feelings are magnified because of his depression." The feelings ebb and flow, however. "It's a challenge loving people with these conditions. There was a time my husband was a registered carer for me because of my condition," she says, and now she makes allowances for his. They navigate carefully around their mental health issues in their household, but it's not simple. "We want things to be on equal terms, but that's not how it always works in practice. Our mental health takes up a lot of room in our relationship." She relates that an ex-partner of hers, someone she'd lived with for a long time, killed himself last year because of his depression. Observing her spouse coping with depression causes her to fear that he may attempt suicide. "You carry fear with you all the time."

Margo says the kind of therapeutic care she receives now in the UK is similarly expensive in South Africa. "Medical aid may pay for some types of care, but it runs out quickly for mental health services. It's harder to get medical aid to pay in South Africa. Familial support has been key, especially for my brother. Mom supports his care, and that has been critical for him." She says her husband's mom has also been supportive, but it's complicated. "His mom is learning to be a counselor, so she's unlearning some things that she did previously. She's more compassionate now, which is helpful." But overall, Margo's husband has struggled more than she has to find community in the UK. He's more reserved and finds it difficult to reach out to others, putting more pressure on Margo to be supportive. She says his mother and she are his primary support system. He hasn't found any local networks of others he can talk with about his struggles.

With her history of sustained trauma in childhood, Margo believes that therapies that take a trauma-informed approach are the most promising. "It has real potential. It takes illness very seriously while not pathologizing patients or seeing them as unhinged. It's helpful when mitigating for harm, especially when doing hard things, like removing children from parents who are harming them. It gives people agency and dignity."

One example of this approach in Margo's experience was when she first met with her current general practitioner. "It was so simple. I told him about my first two experiences with practitioners, the first one who put me on dangerous medication, then the next one who cut me off abruptly. He said, 'That's not ideal, but you're already working through the process of withdrawal. You can either go back on the diazepam and wean off it more slowly, or you can continue on your current course. What do you think you should do?' This was the first time someone had indicated to me that I had a choice. It was the first time someone had approached me with that kind of respect." Margo felt empowered by knowing her doctor was allowing her to make decisions that affected her care. She says it made a huge difference in how she approached her next steps, because they were steps she had chosen. Her doctor's approach implied she had worth.

While Margo believes her C-PTSD is a response to the chaotic environment in her childhood home and her mother's extreme symptoms of mania and depression, she also recognizes the trauma her mother sustained. "I think Mom's early distress is related to all the stressful situations she experienced in her work as an anti-apartheid activist, while she was a young woman and later, as she parented my brother and me. She saw some awful things. There was no language for it, and we didn't know how to debrief. She couldn't come home to us and say, 'this is what I saw today and it was horrific.' She grew up under the apartheid system, and it was brutal. It traumatized her, and because it wasn't processed properly, it was passed on." One of Margo's goals with both her professional work and her work on improving her own mental health is to disrupt the damaging cycles so they're not perpetuated on her children. She's confident that taking a trauma informed approach will help her achieve those goals.

"There's a movement to form a trauma informed task force in the UK, which is promising. There's a briefing paper that is getting a lot of attention and is gaining traction. One of the primary shifts is a focus from asking, 'What's wrong with you?' to asking, "What happened to you?' This new way of thinking shifts blame and perceived toxicity. It's okay to live with illness and distress, but blaming someone for it is nonproductive." She believes that when we stop behaving as though people with a mental illness are toxic, we will be better able to help them live with the illness, while leading productive lives. Instead, the stigma of mental illness makes it difficult for those who live with a diagnosed condition to seek help.

Margo believes that mental health professionals have a role to play in eliminating the stigma, but they have not yet done so. "If there weren't such a stigma around bipolar disorder, my mother would have accepted her diagnosis and cared for it appropriately. The language used when discussing mental illness is unhelpful and stigmatizing." Margo insists that those with mental health conditions can live with their conditions *and* have a good life. Those realities are not mutually exclusive. People need to hear those kinds of assurances from mental health practitioners to destigmatize a diagnosis.

In addition to being a strong proponent of trauma-informed therapies, Margo also sees a great deal of promise in the research of Kimberlé Crenshaw in identifying overlapping and interacting identities. Crenshaw, a law professor and co-founder of the African American Policy Forum, coined the term "intersectionality" to describe, for example, the discrimination faced by individuals because of their various identities. An individual's identity might include labels such as race, class, gender, sexual orientation, or situational factors (Columbia Law School, 2017). Margo explains, "For instance, I'm a white woman who is a migrant in the UK. I have no access to public funds. These are only a few layers of my identity—among others—that must be considered when trying to assess me or provide treatment for my condition." There are stereotypes, or tropes, she says, about hysterical women or drama queens that don't effectively consider all the layers of a woman's individual identity. For males, it's the trope of a strong man who's not allowed to cry or express emotions, or the violent Black man. Tropes don't describe the complexity of a human being, however. "For those engaged in mental health work, it's essential to be conscious of intersectionality and the layers that come together to form an identity."

Seeing and considering the whole person through the context of their experiences and relationships will better inform mental health treatment. Family members play an important role in that perspective as well. According to Margo, mental health practitioners who take the time to assess patients or clients through this lens of intersecting identities can move beyond simple medication prescription. Just managing symptoms is not enough. "Assisting patients in living productive lives while managing potential negative effects of their illness should be the ultimate goal."

4
Sibling stories

Introduction

In most families, siblings share comparable roles as their parents' dependents. There are effects of birth order and temperament. Older children may be responsible for younger siblings to some degree. Younger children may be indulged. Sibling rivalries exist and can lead to serious contentions. However, except for rare exceptions, siblings are subordinate to their parents' authority and subject to the same household standards. In most instances, once siblings are adults, they shoulder little or no responsibility for each other.

Relationships with siblings are generally the longest-lasting associations a person will form throughout their life. Siblings typically outlive their parents. Sibling relationships are well established before partners are chosen or children are born. However, in some ways, our siblings are the people we will always be closest to. Despite the quality or emotional closeness of their bond, siblings share family history, heredity, and longevity (Dunn, 2002).

Margaret had always admired her older sister as wiser and more sophisticated, and then Barb developed schizophrenia. When their parents died, Margaret became Barb's caretaker and has learned patience and an appreciation for ordinary human interactions. For Greg, his mother is still his sister's primary caregiver, but he knows he will one day assume that role. He and his mother work together putting measures in place today to ensure his sister's financial stability in the future, which will make his job easier when the time comes. As the oldest of six children, Sylvia has always felt responsible for her brother, Doug, the youngest child. She and another brother have taken the lead in caring for Doug now that their parents are gone and have resorted to moving Doug to the state with the most beneficial mental health services. Each of these siblings takes seriously their responsibility to advocate for and care for family members, regardless of the strength of their filial bonds.

Margaret

I met Margaret Hawkins through a mutual friend in 2022, just before my memoir was published. Our friend Jan suggested Margaret and I had much in common because we both had a close family member who had been diagnosed with schizophrenia. Margaret was kind enough to read my manuscript and write a blurb (endorsement) for the book jacket. Margaret's own memoir, *How We Got Barb Back: The Story of My Sister's Reawakening After 30 Years of Schizophrenia* (Hawkins, 2010), and a second book, forthcoming from Lived Places Publishing, *At Home With Schizophrenia: One Family's Story* tell her family's story in detail. Since her story has been published, she suggested I use her and her sister Barb's real names when telling their story.

I've read *How We Got Barb Back* twice, which makes me feel I know both sisters well, even though we've never met in person. What I find most striking about Barb's history is the word "reawakening" that appears in the book's title. It documents the story of a viva-cious, intelligent, and socially active young woman whose bright future was cut short by the appearance of angry and threatening voices that soon overtook her consciousness—classic signs of schizophrenia. However, Barb "reawakened" in dramatic fashion when she was 62 years old.

Margaret's memories of Barb, who is 11 years older, before she went to college and before she became ill are a bit hazy. When Margaret started second grade, Barb had already left for the University of Illinois. This may be why she was so determined to understand who her sister was. "I'd come late to the party, and I could never learn enough about Barb, who always seemed to slip out the door just as I was arriving," Margaret says in her book. Instead, she studied photographs of a child she describes as "a dreamy, pretty, dark-haired girl with a willowy figure and a faraway gaze in her big gray stunned-looking eyes." It's in family photos that Margaret found her best clues about who her sister had been.

Barb was the oldest of three children, followed by brother Tom and finally by Margaret, 11 years later. Barb was active in Camp Fire Girls, as evidenced by photos of her with her father at a father-daughter dinner. Barb wore her vest proudly, which was covered in colorful patches. Pictures of Halloween and Christmas gave Margaret the sense that her sister was "always a bit dramatic" but fun. Barb took photos herself when she obtained a camera at around age 11, snapping shots of a slumber party she hosted, the family dog, and "Baby Margaret," among other things. Later photos taken by others demonstrate some sense of her per-sonality. "What strikes me most about these photos now is how cooperative my sister looks, how sweet." By the time Margaret was old enough to really know and remember her sister, Barb had grown older and sharper. She was sometimes "detached and unsmiling" in photos but still vibrant and full of promise. The house seemed a bit empty to Margaret after Barb left for university, but visits home were special events for the whole family. Barb loved her life at college, as illustrated by the stories she told. It's unclear to Margaret now whether Barb was genuinely happy there or beginning to experience troubling symptoms that she shared with no one.

Barb was put on academic probation in 1963, during her sophomore year and moved home to attend a local branch of the university near the family's home. Margaret says she still sometimes tries to recall changes in her sister during this time. She thinks shifts in behavior might have been obvious, but Margaret was still quite young and Barb simply seemed an enchanting, mysterious young woman to her. The fact that she appeared pleased to be living in her childhood bedroom again should have also seemed strange, but Margaret was just glad to have her spirited sister back.

"It wasn't like her at all," Margaret says of her sister's failure to succeed at college, when she'd been so bright and sociable before. "We should have known something was wrong." Then, in 1966, Barb married an Iraqi post-doctoral chemistry student, Karim, whom she'd met at university and who anticipated a future in academia. They lived in Kentucky while he finished his doctoral studies, but he couldn't find suitable employment after graduation. When he secured a chemistry faculty position at a university in Iraq, the couple moved to Basra in 1971. Barb sent frequent letters home from Iraq over the next few years, full of observations of her new life and home. Dramatic changes in the tone of these letters suggested trouble but neither Barb nor Karim ever reported a problem. The couple came back to visit the family in 1974, and it was clear then that something was wrong. Barb's parents blamed her husband and life in Iraq for the change.

The next time Barb and Karim visited the family, he begged Barb's parents to get help for his wife. She would not work, he said, and almost wouldn't get out of bed. Her parents convinced Karim to let Barb stay in the US with them, and he returned to Iraq alone. Afterward, he wrote frequent letters to her father from Iraq, pleading with him to take Barb to a doctor or counselor, to no avail. Karim visited again, but eventually, he sent divorce documents when it appeared that Barb didn't "want to get well" and her parents refused to admit she was ill. Barb settled into her childhood bedroom in her childhood home as a single woman again, apparently undisturbed by the dissolution of her marriage or separation from her husband.

***

After Barb's divorce in 1977, and even after obvious evidence of illness, their father was resistant to seeking medical or psychiatric treatment for her. Margaret's maternal grandmother had committed suicide, and Margaret's mother had suffered bouts of deep depression, so the family was familiar with troubling mental health issues. Her father was leery of anyone being labeled mentally ill, though, and had found medical professionals unhelpful in prior situations. He was skeptical that anything could be done to heal Barb. At the time there really was little to be done, aside from institutionalization and a few rudimentary antipsychotics. Margaret's and Barb's father was determined to protect Barb from what he considered useless, perhaps even cruel, treatment. Their parents tried once to consult a psychiatrist, but the encounter went badly and convinced them that they were the only ones who had Barb's best interests at heart. While Barb lived upstairs, first her mother, and then her father after her mother's death, indulged her by cooking for her and bringing her meals upstairs. He seemed unconcerned that she never left the house and seldom left her bedroom.

Thirty years after Barb's move home and divorce, their father died. It was 2007 and Barb was 62. Margaret suddenly became Barb's caretaker, an eventuality she'd been aware of but hadn't really known how to plan for. The one thing she was committed to was finding help for her sister's condition, but she had no access. Because of Barb's refusal to leave the house, which was now hers to manage, Margaret searched for medical support who would agree to meet Barb at her home.

Fortunately, help appeared, almost as soon as she began reaching out. "It was as though a curtain was drawn, and people would come to the house and say, 'this is what I can do for you,' or 'I can provide that service.' It was incredible." She felt she couldn't have gotten any more assistance than she did. "I was hungry for some kind of help for years and years, but couldn't force any change, because of my father's resistance." Then, when she needed it, help arrived.

Margaret was grateful to find resources almost immediately through an organization in Northfield, Illinois called Wilpower (then the New Foundation Center and now Thresholds). From that agency, she connected with a social worker—Wendy—who was willing to advocate for Barb so that she got the care she needed. From a physician who would visit the home, to a part-time caregiver, to a nurse practitioner, Wendy proved to be a vital resource. "She helped us apply for benefits that Barb qualified for, such as Medicaid, SNAP benefits, and a caregiver through the Illinois Department on Aging. She even found a pharmacy that delivers. Meals on Wheels supplied meals."

Within months, Margaret found professionals who provided psychiatric evaluation and prescribed antipsychotic medication, with startling results. Within a few weeks of taking medication, Barb was functioning much better and the voices receded. She began to interact with people, engaging in limited conversations, something Margaret hadn't witnessed in decades. Her older sister, whom she had admired since childhood literally "reawakened." The change was astonishing.

***

One remarkable element of Barb's story is the delay between the onset of her symptoms and the treatment that controlled them so quickly. From the beginning, Margaret was zealous in ensuring Barb took her medication and set up a system for her to follow, with days of the week and dates marked on her pill minder. Margaret often asked her— sometimes daily—if she'd taken her pill. When it appeared Barb was taking the pills on schedule, she backed off. Recently, though, she was alerted through the social worker, Wendy, who still visits Barb, that she hadn't taken her medication for a few months. After a bit more investigation, they realized Barb had actually not taken any for two *years*.

"At first, I panicked," Margaret says. "But after I calmed down, I realized that Barb had continued to do well in those two years. Her conversation's more rational. I never hear her mention what her voices are telling her anymore. She used to reference her voices and mumble about what they were saying, but she just doesn't do that anymore." Despite no longer taking medication, Barb continues to interact well. She smiles and laughs at jokes; she even tells a few jokes of her own. This was not the case before she received treatment. Margaret finally decided to let go of monitoring the medication. "It seems to me the medication when she first started taking it kickstarted this dramatic change, and she seems to have continued to improve since then." The only thing Barb is treated for now is high blood pressure, and she doesn't seem to mind taking that medication. Aside from letting the visiting nurse do routine assessments, this is the only intervention she's had in decades.

At 81, Barb is doing remarkably well, considering her history, and remains stable, according to Margaret. She has retained the social aptitude she recovered after beginning medication, even though she no longer takes it. This was good news and is consistent with current understanding of her disease. Margaret says she's read that there is now evidence that symptoms of older schizophrenia patients, particularly women, appear to diminish over time.

***

Barb's current caregiver, Yvonne, has been working with her for around 15 years. They're like old friends now, Margaret says of her sister and her caregiver. "Yvonne still goes to the house as many as six days a week to do laundry, buy groceries, and just check on things around the house. I don't know what I'd do without her, but someday she'll retire." The two women enjoy each other's company and often simply watch television or play games together.

Margaret sometimes feels guilty that Barb's life has been so constrained by her condition. She doesn't have friends other than Yvonne, and Wendy when she comes. "Wendy's Jewish, but we celebrate 'Jewish Easter' together every year. She also comes for Barb's birthday." Barb doesn't seem sad about her life at all, though. Margaret recalls when Barb used to be in constant fear. She often talked about the things she feared, things the voices told her to fear. "She would dart away. She wouldn't make eye contact. We couldn't touch her because she was so frightened of our touch." She never talks about the voices or her fears anymore, though, which Margaret believes must be a relief. She now looks people in the eye and lets her sister touch her. She will now smile, whereas she didn't smile in the past. All these improvements came because of the medication she began taking in 2007. "It was actually a low dose then," Margaret says, which increased only slightly over time.

When Wendy asked her once if she wanted any friends, Barb responded, "You're my friend." Margaret wishes her sister had more of a life, but Barb doesn't seem to wish for anything more. On the other hand, being responsible for Barb is somewhat limiting for Margaret. She feels guilty when she travels and can't make her weekly Sunday visit. She recently was awarded an artist's residency in Austria for a month and, while it was a tremendous gift, she was anxious about being gone so long. After she left for Austria, Yvonne was injured by a dog and couldn't come for a while. Although Margaret's husband visited Barb during that time, she still felt guilty. There are other things she'd like to be able to do, but they seem unimportant. "I've built my life around her, but I don't know what else I would have done," Margaret says. "Your life is an infinity of options, so in some ways, having an obligation gives you some kind of structure to build other things around."

Margaret feels rewarded by advocating for her sister's care. "I enjoy being useful. It's great to have someone in your life who can really use your help. This is something I can do. I'm glad to have been able to effectively address Barb's needs."

***

Society's attitudes toward mental health have changed some-what since Barb first became ill, though arguably not enough or in the best ways. Before and during the 1970s, it was common to isolate members of the family with a mental health condition. Her father seemed hesitant to allow much interaction between his older daughter and the outside world, and more so with the mental health community. Margaret teaches college students now, and she finds students in her classes almost clamor to obtain status as "special students." Where once students were horrified at the thought of being labeled as having a disability, things are dif-ferent today. She wonders if things have gone too far. "Today, stu-dents seem to identify with their diagnosis." Students appear to focus on what they can't do, rather than on what they can. While Margaret is accepting of neurodiversity among her students and pleased that people are more open about mental illness, she is uneasy when students seem to embrace the label as though it defines who they are.

That said, Margaret recognizes her students have a right to choose how to identify themselves, just as everyone else does (Mellifont and Smith-Merry, 2021). Neurodiversity describes differences in brain structure and functioning, which are not in themselves disabilities or forms of mental illness. However, students may find that identifying themselves as neurodivergent may facilitate their learning when it allows instructors to accommodate their individual needs in the classroom (Walker, 2014).

When Margaret's memoir first came out more than a decade ago, she did a lot of speaking at conferences and local organizations. She took part in discussions all over the country, and she feels it was helpful to tell her story more broadly and to hear from others. In thinking about policies that benefit individuals with mental illness diagnoses, Margaret emphasizes the importance of a community mental health model. "It's important for the members of smaller, local communities to help the people they know." She sees social workers as critical in connecting to psychiatrists, other medical professionals, and whatever services there are in the community in a more personal way. She doesn't think the community mental health model was ever fully implemented, but there were some options available to Margaret's family. There were services that Barb couldn't or wouldn't take advantage of because she refused to go to group meetings or even to visit physicians. She's rarely left the house in 50 years. "She would never get in the car. Even today, she will only walk outside with me when I take out the trash," Margaret says of her weekly visits to see her sister on Sundays. "Or she'll walk around to the sidewalk, but no further."

Margaret was offered support groups herself, and she attended a few meetings, but she felt she had enough support without them. Still, she is happy those services are available. "Ultimately, the burden is on families, and so many people just live the way Barb did before she was treated. We were fortunate Barb never had violent impulses. Some families deal with worse situations or symptoms than Barb had."

Even though Barb's condition has been stable, Margaret worries about her future. The house Barb lives in needs constant maintenance. It would be traumatic if she had to leave it. Her caregiver, Yvonne, may retire, or other necessary supports might no longer be available. Barb could someday develop a serious physical illness or have an accident in her home. Each of these concerns weighs on Margaret, but the fact that Barb is secure for now is reassuring.

Margaret says she used to write often about incidents in Barb's life just to keep track of them, but she doesn't keep a daily journal. Instead, she has a notebook and finds that writing in it about an incident helps her process it, and that's enough. Overall, her everyday concerns for Barb have diminished, though, because she continues to improve in small ways. Her perspective of the world is fairly normal, according to Margaret, in spite of some odd habits and behaviors. She will answer the phone but won't make a call. Technology is alien to her, so she's stuck in the past in some ways. However, Margaret says Barb's interactions are rooted in reality today, which wasn't the case in the past. She's more sociable than she's been in decades.

"Not long ago, Barb gave me something—a small thing—I don't remember what it was, but when she gave it to me, she said, 'it's a gift.' Barb doesn't give gifts. She never acknowledges my birthday—she just doesn't remember." While Margaret doesn't recall the item itself, she will never forget the impulse Barb had to give her a gift. Her once mysterious older sister has had an incredible journey, and Margaret marvels at how far she's come, the small but significant accomplishments. They are the true gifts.

Greg

"Melody was born with water on the brain—hydrocephalus—and had developmental disabilities her entire life," according to her older brother, Greg. "Borderline personality disorder (BPD) was diagnosed when she was 15 or 16. It took a while to map her moody outbursts to a condition. They knew there were disabilities but they didn't know if there was a disorder associated with them." He doesn't know if there's any connection between the hydrocephalus and the BPD, but because it is also a developmental disorder, he doesn't think it would be surprising.

Greg devotes much of his time and energy to work that he loves. So much so that he considers himself a "workaholic." At the same time, he often spends time responding to his sister's frequent messages and pleas for help. Melody lives in her own condo about an hour away from her brother in Ontario, Canada. Her illness induces a great many mood swings that often require attention from her mother or brother. Greg's mother lives near Melody and meets most of her daughter's everyday needs. However, because their mother is 85 years old, Greg is aware that he will someday become his sister's primary caregiver, just as he is currently the primary support for his partner, Michael, who has been diagnosed with attention deficit hyperactivity disorder (ADHD).

Melody is in her mid-fifties now, a fact that Greg finds astonishing, "given that she smokes almost a pack and a half of cigarettes a day and eats almost nothing but junk food. She subsists on packaged chips." There's a Canadian chain restaurant that specializes in rotisserie chicken, which they serve with a sauce that Greg describes as rich, like rib sauce. "It's just sort of 'calories in a bowl.' When she's done with the chicken she drinks the sauce. I'm just amazed she's still alive, despite her poor eating habits."

Because Melody has always had serious health challenges, there is no real dividing line between her childhood issues and her BPD diagnosis. In her brother's memory, she has always had disabilities. Despite those challenges, or perhaps because of them, Melody can find joy in quite simple things. "Her biggest point of pride is a plaque she received in high school for being the 'most improved'. I'm not sure what she was most improved in, but it really doesn't matter to her." Greg, who is a few years older, says he and his sister are less close than she would like. He describes them as opposites in many ways.

"When I was in grade four, the school wanted me to skip grades five and six and go directly to grade seven. And my parents said no, but I took enrichment courses and transferred to a French school. I was just thrown into a complete immersion type program and then took all the advanced high school programs available through high school. In that sense, we were diametric opposites." Greg describes Melody as the most generous person in the world, but he can get frustrated by her impatience and her need to have things repeated and explained.

"It's frustrating that she wants to be my best friend. She adulates me as her big brother, looks up to me. But we have little in common outside of our familial relationship." Melody is very religious, which Greg is not. Greg is gay, and she is not. "She absolutely loves Michael, who has been my partner for 32 years, but she has all these strictures of her religion that relate to being gay. She bursts with pride when she talks about me and I burst with pride whenever I talk about her, too, because she's so generous. She's very, very giving." Despite her obvious love for him and for Michael, he says she will occasionally have a meltdown and say absolutely horrid and hurtful things to them about the physicality of being gay. That can be hard to overlook. "So there's that, and there's the absolute depths of depression. Half the conversations I have with her are her saying, 'I hate myself. I want to kill myself.' She's wanted to kill herself since she was 15. She's never attempted suicide, though, because she's terrified of pain."

Her fear of pain doesn't keep her from talking about suicide, however. Greg says she will check herself into a crisis center or the hospital overnight when she feels that way. "Her depression is blown out of all proportion sometimes." He says the service people at the crisis center and hospital know her, so they know how to respond. "They give her some attention and help her calm down. Time is the healer more than anything else. On the other hand, I have trouble responding. She will text me that she is so depressed. I respond that I'm not a mental health professional." He tells her that he doesn't have a solution and that he's sorry she feels so bad, but he doesn't have a band aid for what hurts. He suggests she seek appropriate professional mental health care instead. She has therapy providers, but she instead contacts her brother when she's feeling depressed.

Melody lives in a small town, about five minutes away from their mother, and Greg lives in Toronto, about an hour away. He says that's another way in which he and his sister are unlike each other. "She lives in an auto assembly town outside the city. We grew up not far from there, but I couldn't wait to escape. It's a blue collar town that thrives around auto workers, which I found a little rough around the edges." His sister, on the other hand, is steeped in that life and loves her surroundings. It provides Melody's mental health services, for which he is thankful.

Aside from the basic national health system for medical services, Canada has provincial mental health systems. "There have been announcements of national disability supports, but those have not emerged. It's an ongoing situation. There was a bill passed a couple of years ago, but it keeps getting tabled and revised. While that may help immensely, until then, the provinces are responsible for providing services." As a result, the Ontario disability support program (ODSP) provides a monthly stipend for those who are considered unemployable and operates separately from the national employment insurance system. ODSP is not related to employment, but it's tied to income. Melody qualifies because she is deemed permanently unemployable. Greg is grateful for this program, but her unemployed status is a concern for other reasons. "This is the reason she gets bored all the time and has no significant joy in her life. Without a job, she doesn't know what to do with herself much of the time." He says she applies for jobs, and while he is doubtful she'll be hired, applying does occupy some of her time.

ODSP provides some security for Melody, but it's not enough to cover the total of her expenses. "We've been topping her off every month. That's how she lives. That supplemental money mostly comes from my mother." He says Melody has a big fear that after their mother is gone and Greg becomes her caregiver, her finances will suffer. "She doesn't fully trust me, no matter how often I reassure her. When our father was alive, our parents bought her a condo because she had trouble in the past getting into fights with neighbors and she'd get evicted from her apartment. Now she can't get evicted, at least not as easily. She owns the property … or the three of us co-own it: our mom, me, and Melody." Greg's father died several years ago.

Even though she has a place to live, Melody spends most of her time with a gentleman who's about 20 years older than she is. "She calls him her fiancée sometimes, but they're not official. His house is a ten-minute walk from hers and she spends six nights a week at his place. She'd probably be there seven if it didn't mean she'd lose her benefits." The ODSP benefits are dependent on the recipient maintaining their own residence. In addition, if an ODSP recipient is imprisoned for more than 30 days at a time, they lose benefits for life. Hence, Melody has to be careful about her interactions with police, which have been a problem in the past, due to anger management problems. "She's been good for the past 15 years. Her medication has helped keep her within a stable range, so there have been no recent issues." When their father was alive, he and their mother would accompany Melody to court when she had been arrested or involved in an altercation.

They would acknowledge her infraction and the need for penalty, but they would plead with the judge not to administer a sentence of more than 30 days and were successful each time.

Greg also describes a disability tax credit program that his mom takes advantage of as her daughter's caregiver. Greg may become his sister's caregiver after their mother's death, but he currently receives the deduction on Michael's behalf and can't take more than one deduction.

In addition to these benefits, the family participated in the registered disability support program, a deposit matching program up to $40K. It was $15, 000 in the first year and another $1,000 could be matched each year, terminating at $40K on Melody's 40th birthday. "Until then, we matched funds in that account. Contributions weren't taxed when they went into the account, but will be taxed when they're taken out." These financial programs have helped provide the family peace of mind for Melody's future care.

"Last week, though, Melody saw an advertisement from a company purporting to do the legwork of filling out the tax credit forms, including talking to the Canada Revenue Agency (the equivalent of the US Internal Revenue Service), her doctors, and other mental health professionals on her behalf to fill out the forms to enroll her in the program. She signed up with them and gave them all sorts of personal information, including her social insurance number. She gave them authorization to act for her. We're trying to get her out of this agreement now. It's a scam. They claim 30% of every benefit received, when there is in reality no cost to apply. She just didn't understand that she was already enrolled in the program."

Another recent incident contributes to Greg's frustration with his sister. "She's subject to scams, and because she lives apart from the family, we don't always know what she's seeing or falling prey to. She got scammed a few years ago when she had Mom driving her to stores all around town, but she wouldn't tell Mom what she was doing. Scammers wanted her to buy Apple gift cards. She was buying quantities of gift cards, and because she couldn't get enough at one place, she was having Mom drive her from one to another. We finally figured it out after she'd spent $3,500 on them."

Melody's tendency to be susceptible to the lure of money is troubling. Greg says they're investigating better systems to prevent these scammers from taking advantage of her in the future. "There's a guardianship for property legal certification we can file for. We're in the early stages of applying to have Mom and me appointed her guardians of property. It's like power of attorney, but in this case, it renders her signature invalid on contracts." Because of their mother's age, he feels obligations for both his mother and sister. In addition, he is the sole wage earner in his family, so he's caring for three people: his mom, Melody, and Michael. The responsibility can feel heavy sometimes.

Aside from Melody's financial benefits, she also has a psychiatrist who prescribes medication and a social worker who helps her navigate programs. It took 20 years to find effective medication, according to Greg. They tried drugs that made her too tired, or grumpy, or made her skin itch. "The cocktail they give her now seems to be working. She still gets depressed, but her moodiness, like extreme anger, is much more restrained than in the past." Her family has encouraged her to consult the social worker for talk therapy as well, but she hasn't done that so far.

One financial benefit that Greg believes is a novel approach is the Passport Program attached to the ODSP. It allows generous funds each year toward expenses for entertainment or educational activities. "Mom and Melody might travel to Ottawa on the train, spend the night in a hotel, and attend a concert or a play, and the Passport Program provides a rebate for their trip. Both of their tickets are covered for the outing, so it benefits them both."

In addition to the ODSP and its associated programs, caregivers receive a nonrefundable tax credit to offset their tax liability. Greg's father received it until his death seven years ago, and now their mother gets it. "It's peace of mind for her. When Melody's 65, she can draw from it like a pension. She qualifies for old age security at 65 as well." While this is another reassuring benefit, "We're concerned she will withdraw money to give away. She's too generous." National and provincial financial benefits like these are much appreciated and provide a measure of stability.

***

If there is emotional or networking support available to families of those with mental health conditions, Greg is not aware of it. He suspects there might be some, but he isn't sure where to look for it. "They're not well advertised if they exist. I haven't seen anything aimed at family, other than those programs absolving financial concerns, and those are a relief in themselves." He doesn't know his sister's professional caregivers, though he is sure his mother does. He recently discovered and connected with Melody's social worker on social media. This connection may be important in the future if his mother is suddenly unable to oversee his sister's care.

Greg doesn't believe there are sufficient efforts made by mental health professionals to integrate family members into the care of those who have mental health conditions. He describes a two-tier health system in terms of mental health. Canada's national health system provides for core health care and will recommend a clinical psychologist or psychiatrist. But Greg believes the mental health services are inadequate unless a patient is willing to pay for private care. For Melody, and for Greg's partner Michael, this is the care they receive. Greg says they are fortunate in being able to afford to do so..

Even so, a patient's family isn't well-integrated into care. For example, Michael sees a psychiatrist who has never invited Greg to participate in their sessions. Not long ago, when Greg was in the process of applying for benefits for Michael, he communicated with the psychiatrist and shared observations about Michael's challenges with ADHD that he doesn't believe the psychiatrist was aware of. "He was only hearing Michael's side of the story and nothing outside his own perception. I wanted him to understand the impact his condition has on his everyday life." That proved helpful, but there's been nothing else in 20 years of care. "You would think they'd want to build a relationship with the family, but they haven't reached out."

After our conversation, Greg did some online research and reached out to say he'd located the Ontario Caregiver Organization, which provides supports to caregivers that he hadn't been aware of. He asked them a few questions and found that they provide peer support and counseling for caregivers, as well as numerous tools and links to other resources in the community. Although he told me that he didn't have time to take advantage of support groups or networking at the moment, he may find comfort in knowing that such programs exist if he needs them in the future, as he takes on a more active role in caregiving for Melody.

Several years ago, Greg was successfully treated for cancer and found a lot of helpful support for his medical condition through the hospital where he received treatment. He doesn't take advantage of them since he's been in remission. However, he appreciated that they reached out with a survey to ensure he had received good care. They inquired about the care he received, with respect to gender identity and sexual health. It was gratifying to be asked. He would like to see similar concern for the quality of care his sister and partner have received.

***

The psychiatrist Michael had been seeing recently retired, and since then his general practitioner has taken a more active role in managing his medication dosage. This doctor now expects Michael to see him monthly, which has been a great improvement, and something the psychiatrist never requested. They may only have a brief check-in, but that regular visit has been significant. The medication is still not optimized, but it's getting better. "He's in better hands now. He's on a waitlist for another psychiatrist and I've encouraged him to see a social worker as well. I think talk therapy would be helpful." Greg says Michael gets very frustrated when he can't accomplish what he wants to, as a result of his ADHD. "He's very intelligent, but he can't organize or prioritize some of the things he's intellectually capable of. He just can't get them completed. Once they get the medication dosage right, he might be able to take greater control over his life." Greg says his mother has sometimes suggested that he should leave Michael, due to his mental health issues. Greg responds by asking if she would leave Melody because of her condition, and of course his mother says no. "It's no different for me with Michael. I've taken vows, for better or worse. I have no reason to break that vow. He's taking his medication and doing what he needs to do."

Greg doesn't think Michael would benefit from support groups or other community networking, because of his reserved personality, but he seems to draw support from online groups and sites that help him feel like he's not alone. "Commonality is helpful. He can see that it's not him that's the problem, it's the disorder. The problem can be named: executive dysfunction." There's a certain relief in naming it and recognizing that others have the same problem. Michael exhibits a high degree of self-awareness in this regard that Melody lacks. According to Greg, "Melody's problem is overconfidence, and Michael's is underconfidence."

Just as Greg is faithful in his commitment to Michael, his responsibility to Melody is ingrained. "I tell her I can't be there every time she wants me, but when she truly needs me, I am there." Many years ago, when their father was still alive, Melody was thrown out of an apartment she was sharing with a boyfriend. They were fighting and she had to move out in one day. "Dad and I rented a truck and met at her apartment to move her out that very day. When I remind her of this, she agrees I have been there for her in the past."

According to Greg, Melody often confuses what she wants with what she needs. What she *wants* can sometimes be overwhelming. "Mom bears the brunt of it now, and I get the overflow. We're looking at getting control of her finances and property to keep her sustained. She'll have to take care of her own happiness, but everything else we're putting in place for her will keep her financially secure."

Meanwhile, one activity that Melody is enormously proud of is her fundraising activity for a nonprofit organization called Community Care Durham, which provides a wide range of mental health support in Durham, Ontario, such as adult day programs, assisted living, meals on wheels, exercise classes, and much more. Greg's not sure if Melody uses any of their services, but she has been fundraising for them for 18 years. "She increases the amount raised every year and takes immense pride in that. They give her a little gift each year—maybe a T-shirt or something—and she is always delighted with whatever they give her. I am very proud of her for taking part in the annual fundraiser. She's truly the most generous person I know."

Sylvia

When I ask what her younger brother, Doug, was like as a child, Sylvia tells me it's hard to remember him before his personality changed so dramatically and because of their age difference. However, she laughs when she recalls one memory of her brother. "He was a young entrepreneur. Our house in Virginia was down a dirt road, off a very hilly road. Cars would lose hubcaps coming down the hill. Doug scooped them up and put them up on a board at the end of our street with a sign: *Hubcaps For*

Sale—A Dollar Apiece. He was always looking for ways to make money."

Sylvia is the oldest, and Doug the youngest of 6 children. "Dad was an Air Force pilot. When Doug was not quite two years old and I was almost 12, Dad decided to go to Vietnam. He didn't have to go, but he wanted to go. This meant leaving Mom and six kids back in California, where we lived at the time. Until Dad left, I hadn't noticed how much Mom drank, but I think I realized for the first time that she was an alcoholic. As the oldest, I would feed everyone and put them to bed."

With their father gone and their mother unavailable because she was so often under the influence of alcohol, Doug didn't have ordinary parental relationships. Sylvia says, "We sometimes wonder if Doug suffered from Fetal Alcohol Syndrome. He didn't do as well in school as the rest of us, and once I realized how often Mom abused alcohol, I wondered if that was the case during her pregnancy with Doug." Sylvia left home after high school, when Doug was still in elementary school and doesn't have as many memories of him in the years after she left.

When Doug was 18 and a senior in high school, he got his girlfriend pregnant, and they had a daughter. They married, then lived with either his parents or her parents and had a second daughter before they divorced. "Sometime in there, they were smoking a lot of pot and then got involved with crack cocaine. So they had two kids, and this was not okay at all." Eventually, Sylvia's sister took their nieces, and the family went to court to try to gain custody of them. Sylvia says she lived overseas during this period and isn't sure what happened next. In any event, Doug had the younger daughter and his ex-wife had the older for a while. "Each parent took a child."

"When I came back from overseas, Doug was exhibiting clear signs of schizophrenia: delusions and hallucinations." He was around 25 at the time and staying at their parents' house while their parents were vacationing. "He was using Windex to spray the 'ghosts' that were bothering him. He said he knew he wasn't crazy, because the family dog saw them, too." Sylvia says the family tried an intervention at that point and spoke with everyone they could think of about having him committed, but there was nothing they could do unless he got violent. "We had no luck getting help for him in Virginia. The law wouldn't allow it without his permission."

Doug moved down to Texas for a short time to live with another brother and took his daughter with him. "He had to come back to Virginia because his wife was suing him for custody. Shortly after that, our brother in Texas died suddenly of lung cancer, when he was 39. That affected Doug hugely."

Their parents retired and moved to Hilton Head, South Carolina. Doug moved with them. His daughter was then living with her other grandmother. Not long after moving to South Carolina, Doug mistakenly went into the wrong bank to get cash from his account. "When they didn't give him money as he expected, he made a scene. The bank called my parents and the police, and my dad met them at the bank. The police suggested there was a judge who had a lot of experience with similar situations and who could get them some help. The laws in South Carolina were different from Virginia and allowed them to get Doug in a state psychiatric hospital in Columbia. Mom and Dad lived about four hours away but visited him there on the weekends." While he was hospitalized, Doug received his first psychiatric diagnosis of paranoid schizophrenia.

The psychiatrist who treated Doug referred to his schizophrenia as "latent," Sylvia says, because of Doug's relatively late age at diagnosis: 26 or 27. Boys with schizophrenia typically show symptoms in their late teens. "He said Doug's psychosis might not have presented itself, but that the crack cocaine put him over the edge." The antipsychotic medication Doug took seemed to work well enough and Doug improved.

After he left the hospital, he wanted to live independently, so he secured subsidized housing and moved into his own place. "It didn't go well. At one point, Doug got beat up so badly, Mom and Dad brought him back to live with them. His jaw was broken and wired shut. We think maybe he got beat up for money or the drugs that he was probably using and maybe selling. Doug would never say. By this time, Mom and Dad were older, and Doug was hard for them to handle. He was addicted to drugs, cigarettes, and sex. It got to the point that he would ask my dad for $20 so he could get a blow job. That was hellish for my parents, but at least Doug was safe."

Doug was still seeing a psychiatrist regularly and taking his medications, according to Sylvia. Doug's and her parents' living situation was not healthy for any of them, but they didn't want to change anything. "Every year or so, I would do some research to find Doug a place to live but I had no support." Then Doug started stealing from their parents. "Dad had gone to West Point, and they got married right after he graduated. Mom had a West Point engagement ring that went missing. Dad's coin and stamp collections, a lot of Mom's jewelry, and silverware all disappeared. I checked all the nearby pawn shops but couldn't find anything. Doug had sometimes been involved with women who exchanged sex for whatever he could give them." She says Doug was also forging checks on their father's checking account for outrageous amounts, like $10,000. "My parents were at their wits' end. Dad threatened to cut Doug out of his will, but instead, our brother Richard, who is the second oldest, and I convinced Dad to create a trust. This was in 2018.

"One of the times when Doug had stolen a lot from my parents, Dad called the police and said he was going to teach Doug a lesson." Sylvia was visiting from her home in Virginia at the time. "My dad's doing this like it's going to teach Doug a lesson to be put in jail overnight. I was beside myself, but I packed up all Doug's medications. I explained Doug's situation to the officers. I asked them not to handcuff him with his hands behind his back, told them Doug gets carsick, all this stuff. The sheriff said, 'you know, we don't have to take him,' but my dad was saying, 'no, you do.' So they took him. We got him out of jail the next day—they hadn't given him his medication. When I got home from that trip, I was so sick. I had pushed so much down, and I just lost it. You read about people with schizophrenia and their encounters with police, and it scared the shit out of me. I was so pissed at my father for even considering that this was a good thing to do."

***

"When Mom was 78, Dad was hit by a truck while riding his bicycle. He was in the hospital afterwards, and Mom almost drank herself to death. This was during the brief period when Doug was living on his own, and we had all been trying to call her but didn't get an answer. We asked Doug to go check on her. He found her passed out, almost comatose from alcohol poisoning. He was traumatized by that. Mom spent a week in ICU and stopped drinking after that—a good outcome for a scary situation. After that, we would give her a nonalcoholic beer, and she was satisfied with that."

Sylvia's mom developed dementia in her eighties, and the family hired caregivers to help take care of her. "While Mom didn't drink any more, she was still smoking. It used to scare the crap out of me, because here was my 87-year-old mother trying to light a cigarette and maybe burn the house down. As her dementia worsened, though, it was like she forgot to smoke. It was wild."One of the caregivers they hired, Paula, had once been a house cleaner for her parents. Sylvia and her siblings soon discovered that Paula was taking advantage of their parents and brother. "The other caregivers would tell us they found used condoms in my father's bedroom, just yucky stuff. We don't really know what she was doing with Doug. To be fair, Doug would tell us stuff, but he has schizophrenia. I believe about a third of what he tells me. He's good at using part fiction and part reality. We didn't learn until later that Paula was telling Dad we wanted to take advantage of him and said she would protect him from us."

Sylvia's mom died in 2019. "Despite an often contentious relationship with her, Doug was devastated by her death."The COVID pandemic came the next year, and things basically shut down. It meant Sylvia and her siblings had less opportunity to see their father and brother and to monitor the caregivers, including Paula. "We couldn't go anywhere. Dad and Doug both stopped taking their medications consistently. One day, one of their caregivers called me and said he came to see my dad but Doug wouldn't let him in the house. He said, 'Doug told me that his dad was fine and didn't want to see me. I could see your dad trying to get up off the couch, but he couldn't get up on his own.' We called an ambulance." Sylvia says her dad was very sick at that point. He was admitted to the hospital, leaving Doug home alone, not a good situation, according to Sylvia. She and her brother Richard called the police and Doug's psychiatrist to try to get Doug out of the house and admitted to the psych unit while their dad was in the hospital. When the police got to the house, Doug told them that he was fine and was taking his medication, so they left. They couldn't do anything. Sylvia and Richard have durable power of attorney, but he would not agree to give them the power to make his medical decisions. "We couldn't force anything, but the next day, Doug called an ambulance for himself. So both Dad and Doug were in the same hospital in Hilton Head."

After Sylvia's dad was released from the hospital, he moved to an assisted living facility in Savannah. Paula had been a caregiver up to this point, and she was becoming hostile. "Mostly, I was trying to separate them both from Paula's influence. We were hearing disturbing stories that we couldn't confirm. When Dad was in rehab, Paula showed up there and told staff she had power of attorney. She wanted to be involved with his medical decisions, and he was agreeing with her. She would call me and say there would be a special place in hell for me because I was denying my father the care he needed." Sylvia's dad got settled into assisted living and Sylvia reported Paula to authorities in both South Carolina and Georgia, but she doesn't think any action was taken against her.

While Doug was still in the psychiatric hospital, Sylvia got a call from his nurse to say they planned to discharge him in two days, a week earlier than planned. "It was very frustrating that they wouldn't really say why they were discharging him." Sylvia and Richard had arranged for Doug to move to a group home in Savannah, near their father, but the home didn't have a place for him immediately. Everything was complicated because of COVID, and it was difficult to find a placement that quickly. They had to put Doug in the memory care unit of the facility where their father was until the group home could take him. "It was a bed, though," Sylvia said, then laughed. "He was ordering pizza from there a couple of times a week." He moved to the group home as soon as they had room.

Less than a year later, Sylvia's dad died. "In April of 2021, the nurse from his facility called to say she didn't think he would live much longer. My husband and I went to Harrisonburg to get a COVID vaccine and were on our way home when she called. We drove down a couple of days later. Richard and his wife also came. Doug didn't want to see Dad that whole time, even though he was nearby. Dad died about 10 days after we got there. He was lucid when we got there; he wasn't at the end.

"While Doug was in Savannah, we used to talk to him regularly, but then it was less and less. We bought Doug a phone but found out he'd called to get food stamps from the state of West Virginia and called to apply for Medicaid, even though he already had it. He was on the phone all the time, so we had to take his phone away and then we couldn't talk with him at all. In the summer of 2023, we heard from the nurse who checked on Doug occasionally." She said she was concerned because the people at the group home wouldn't let her see Doug anymore. Sylvia and Richard decided to move Doug to another group home closer to where Richard lives in Atlanta. When Richard went to get Doug, he was shocked to realize that the woman in charge of the group home had stopped taking Doug to get his monthly shots. Doug had also lost about 100 pounds. He looked terrible. I don't think they were feeding him," Sylvia says. Doug was moved into the new group home about two years ago and Sylvia says he's doing well.

"It's amazing what people will do to vulnerable people if they think they can," Sylvia says. "They were collecting money from Doug's Social Security, his disability benefits, and Medicaid, but he wasn't getting good care."

Doug is now 57 and was diagnosed two years ago with early onset dementia. "When he was in Savannah, my husband and I would go down to visit and take him out to dinner or lunch, which he loves." Now that he's in Atlanta, she says Richard sees him more regularly. He and his wife bring him to their home, where Richard's in-laws and adult daughter also live. Those are hectic, busy times with a houseful of people, which Sylvia describes as healthy for Doug. "I'm very impressed with the group home he is in now. It is clean, and the caretakers are available. They take him to church every Sunday. They ensure he gets his medications.

The wife of the couple who runs the group home is a registered nurse. She became concerned several months ago that Doug's talk was getting too sexual in nature. "According to Doug, he's fathered about a hundred children with famous women," Sylvia says with a chuckle. In response, Doug's psychiatrist changed his prescription. "Medication is tricky, though," Sylvia says, "and we've all noticed a difference in his behavior. He now has a phone and will call me and Richard and one of my sisters on Saturdays to talk. Conversations with him can be wild. He always wants to talk to my kids, but they're adults now and out of the house. He insists I'm keeping them from him and gets mad at me, but he just can't remember they've grown up." Sylvia also says the stories Doug tells her in those calls are a mix of truth and fantasy, which makes it hard to take much of what he says seriously. Despite that, she appreciates the weekly communication.

***

Sylvia recognizes that individuals with mental illness have rights, and she supports their right to make informed choices. "But Doug lies with conviction, and I'm amazed at the number of mental health professionals who believe what he tells them." She says it would be helpful if providers checked in with family members who know the patient well enough to corroborate their stories. "Doug's right to make decisions is important, but I can't get him help if he won't accept it. Even with durable power of attorney, I can't make his medical decisions. If Doug can be convinced of what he needs, everything is fine, but it depends on his mood."

Dealing with a family member who needs so much attention can be exhausting. "I've been in therapy myself for more than

35 years," Sylvia says. She knows there are services available to family members through the National Alliance on Mental Illness (NAMI), but she hasn't taken advantage of them. "Dad was involved with NAMI for a while and supported it heavily. When he died, it was one of the causes we suggested for remembrance gifts in his obituary." However, it was difficult to navigate services during COVID, when Doug's situation was so tenuous. "There really wasn't any guidance from the mental health staff we dealt with." She is still astounded that the hospital Doug was in for treatment during the COVID-19 lockdown was simply going to release him with little warning. She believes the staff should have had more awareness of Doug's situation and empathy for him. "Stuff like that, you don't need to do. He would have ended up on the street or back in the hospital. Even now, he doesn't take his meds on his own. His caregivers make sure he takes it."

In addition, Sylvia believes law enforcement personnel should be better trained in dealing with people who have mental health challenges. "Doug's night in jail might not have scared the shit out of him, but it did a number on me." If he'd been there any length of time, she's afraid he might have died. "He would have been killed, because he talks." She also has experience with caregivers and others taking advantage of the people in their care. "I think abuse happens all too frequently." Sylvia would like to see more vetting and oversight of those employees. She appreciates the group home concept in Georgia, in homes where seniors, individuals with disabilities, or others with Medicaid who have special needs can live and receive care. "Where he is now, he goes out twice a week for an all-day program, which is nice."

Sylvia has been a consistent advocate for her brother and active in finding suitable living arrangements for him. "As the oldest child, I've felt responsible in a way for all my siblings, and especially for Doug, since he's the youngest. All his life I've advocated for him." She has also supported Doug's interests with mental health professionals, nurses and doctors at the hospitals, law enforcement, and neighbors. She has participated in a few of Doug's sessions with his psychiatrist. She has all of Doug's medical records but has no rights when it comes to therapy sessions and Doug doesn't welcome her involvement.

Sylvia's siblings are spread out in Colorado, Ohio, Georgia, Virginia, and at one time, Texas. "When we were looking for a good place for Doug to live, we researched mental health law in all those places." She says none of the states provided what she would consider ideal policies, but Colorado seemed the best option. "One of my sisters lives there. However, Doug thought it was too cold and wouldn't go." Sylvia thinks it's unfortunate they were forced to resort to choosing Doug's living arrangements based on which state had the better mental health services. "It's a shame services aren't universally beneficial for families like ours. But here we are."

5
Partner stories

Introduction

Of the four family relationships explored in this book, life partnerships are the most dependent on individual personality and experience, adjusted by societal expectations. While we are inextricably linked by genetics to our parents, children, and siblings, there is no such link between romantic partners. Intimate partnerships require deliberate and consistent effort to maintain and are thus susceptible to dissolution. Choosing to stay in such a union requires compromise and collaboration between adults with equal status in a household, even if responsibilities are unevenly divided.

When one partner is diagnosed with a mental illness, both partners must restructure their roles in the relationship. The unaffected partner is left with greater family responsibility and may be required to assume obligations they are uncomfortable with, causing stress for both partners and for any children in the household. A research study published in *Curationis* identified four categories of complications introduced into a marriage when one partner has a mental illness: altered social roles, emotional upheaval, interpersonal distance, and a changed relationship with self (Mokoena, 2019).

The stories in this section illustrate only a few examples of these changes. Patricia was unable to reconcile the damage her husband's delusions were causing their family and with being shut out of any discussion regarding his treatment. Despite her ongoing commitment to their marriage vows and to his well-being, she found it impossible to continue in the marriage. Samy, on the other hand, has been a constant cheerleader for his wife's mental wellness and a devoted partner in encouraging her to maintain effective treatment for more than two decades. The youngest of those I interviewed, Celeste sometimes finds herself acting as her partner's therapist, a role she is uneasy with but finds workable because of her conscious efforts to "pour into herself." One common element in these stories is the seriousness with which each individual takes the well-being of their partner, despite the challenges of mental illness.

Patricia

When Patricia met Charles, one of the things that attracted her to him was his dedication to a military career. Charles's father had been career military, and Charles respected his dad greatly. He intended to spend his career in the same way as his father. Patricia's childhood hadn't been easy, and a future with a young military man promised security. "He would take good care of me, I thought, and we would build a stable home," she says.

Charles was in military navigation training in Louisiana when they met and was popular with the other students. They would get together socially sometimes, and Patricia enjoyed joining in when she could. Aside from being an Auburn University football fan, Patricia didn't know of any other interests or hobbies. A military career seemed his only ambition.

The couple married in 1970, when they were 21. "I was a hippie before I met Charles," Patricia says, "and I went from marching in protests to sitting demurely in military wives' teas after we married." The transition was a bit difficult, but Patricia was happy. Then four months later, Charles went to serve in Vietnam. "He flew World War II planes and had top security clearance. I never knew details, because he didn't talk about his missions while he was there," Patricia says. "But the experience changed him."

Still, Patricia was pleased with her situation. She and Charles had a daughter in 1972, then a son in 1978. The family traveled together when they had the time and Patricia kept busy with the children. However, she was learning that Charles did not easily take advice from anyone. He insisted on doing things his way and didn't respond well to suggestions—hers or anyone else's.

In order to receive military retirement pay, Charles needed to serve 20 years, and that's what he did. "But he wasn't successful," Patricia says. "He never advanced in rank the way his father had." It caused him to become cynical, and the family paid a price for his unhappiness. Patricia believes his experiences in Vietnam and bitterness at a failed career contributed to his illness. She thinks this may have been the beginning of his delusions.

After Charles retired, he became very politically active, according to Patricia. He wrote dozens and dozens of letters to their congressmen. "Our long-distance phone bill was astronomical," Patricia says. "He was calling Washington, D.C. all the time." Looking back, she thinks these were early signs of delusional disorder, a condition on the schizophrenia spectrum that he eventually developed. He never had hallucinations, but his delusions had so convinced him of their truth that it threatened their family's well-being. Still, Patricia made the best of things. After retirement, he chose a second career selling stocks and bonds, which wasn't very lucrative either. Because his income wasn't dependable, Patricia worked hard, using her psychology degree, to fill the gaps. The family still traveled when they could and enjoyed seeing new sights. Her daughter has better memories of early times together than her son, though. Charles was in better spirits during her early childhood. "My son says he never had a relationship with his dad."

The intensity of Charles's instability didn't become clear until one evening when he and Patricia were out to dinner and Charles announced, "I'm going to be President." His statement took Patricia by surprise, but she soon realized that he meant it literally. "I think I already knew something was wrong, but it wasn't until he said he would be president—without any kind of plan or projection of how that might come to be—that I admitted to myself he was seriously ill." She soon realized he'd shared delusions with others who suspected that something was wrong, but he didn't do anything about it and didn't confide his suspicions to her. At that point, she encouraged him to seek help, but her efforts were unsuccessful. Patricia says the family had attended church together for many years, where she had served for a time as church administrator. The pastor she worked with had a daughter with mental illness and he was instrumental in helping Charles get help. "He approached me one day about what he'd observed and said he knew Charles needed help." Because he wouldn't listen to Patricia, and she knew her husband trusted the pastor, they planned a family intervention in which his father and their pastor were able to finally convince him to admit himself to the hospital for treatment.

He was in and out of the hospital several times after that, but Patricia says that his doctors wouldn't share medical information with her because Charles hadn't authorized it. "That was the most infuriating thing about the situation. I lived with him and had to deal with his behaviors and try to shield the children from them, but I wasn't allowed to help make decisions for his treatment. All I could do was pray. I prayed the Serenity Prayer a lot during those days." Serenity didn't come.

Eventually, Charles's delusions became destructive to their family and their relationships with friends and extended family. Their daughter had graduated from high school and moved off to college, but their son was still at home. "I considered filing for divorce but talked it over with our son before taking action." While he didn't have a good relationship with his dad, he was worried about the immediate disruption a divorce would cause. "He asked me to promise him two things: that I would keep my married name, and that I would wait to move to California as I planned to do until he was out of high school." Patricia agreed.

From 1989 to 1992, Patricia says she just barely kept herself together. "I almost lost a job once because of the stress," she says. A trained psychologist, Patricia had been a case manager for a nonprofit but was dealing with her husband's disorder so much it interfered with her work.

"I was even called into a congressman's office once. He told me, 'Your husband is stalking my aide. Get him out of here.'" Still, no one seemed to want to listen to how her husband's destructive behavior was affecting the family, Patricia says. She was eventually let go from her job as a case manager and found another at an adult day care center. "About six weeks after I was hired, my boss underwent mastectomy surgery, and I had to basically run the center on my own." But she was determined to keep a roof over their heads and support the family.

In 1992, Patricia filed for divorce. She found a lawyer who ensured that she would be secure. "She didn't fight for child support, as so many attorneys do," she says. "Both of the kids were grown by then anyway. What she did was fight for my right to a sizable portion of his retirement pay. That made all the difference." She describes her attorney as a wonderfully compassionate advocate for her and the children's best interests. "God gives you what you need."

When Patricia's and Charles's divorce was final, the family had been in Texas for several years. It was Charles's terminal assignment with the military, and he retired there. Though neither Charles nor Patricia was from Texas originally, they stayed on because the children had deep roots there. Patricia did go back to California for a time, but she, Charles, their children and their children's families are in Texas still.

One day, while Patricia was dealing with the aftermath of Charles's undoing and the divorce, someone shot into a crowd at the White House and the story was that the man who did it was mentally ill. His wife was quoted in one of the reports Patricia read, and she found herself in tears for what the wife had endured. She began a poem that day dedicated to the wife. It began:

I've prayed for you for three days now
We're just two women who've never met
Most would say we have little in common
I say we have too much.

"Everyone handles things differently," Patricia says, about the trauma the family has undergone. "Our daughter was the only one who could talk her father into anything. She was the only one who could talk him down when he was caught up in a delusion. He listened to her." While she was away at college, though, her dad fell apart and their daughter seemed to blame her mother for not holding things together. "It caused a rift in our relationship," Patricia says. "We're still rebuilding it today, and it's much better, but it's because we're both working hard at it."

As is true in most families, her daughter and son have quite different personalities and temperaments; they respond to their family's situation in different ways. Patricia considers their son "brilliant". He graduated summa cum laude with a degree in Information Technology from Rice University in Houston. He was always highly competitive in school, and Patricia suspects he needed to prove his mental wellness to himself, in contrast to his father's mental illness.

After the divorce, Patricia enjoyed reconnecting with family in California, but she made frequent trips back to Texas to see her children. When her daughter discovered she was pregnant with triplets, though, Patricia decided it was time to return to Texas permanently. She's glad she did and now enjoys her daughter's three children and her son's two, all of whom are adults now.

Her son's wife and he have been friends since they were fourteen. Patricia's daughter-in-law's mother has bipolar disorder. "I think the reason they became such good friends was because they both had parent problems that not everyone knew about." She thinks that formed a bond between them. It was hard for her family to talk about mental illness, especially during the years when the children were young and self-conscious, but she believes her son and his girlfriend gave each other some comfort in knowing they had similar situations.

Several years ago, Charles was taken in by a scam and gave up his home and car to a woman he believed was trustworthy. Someone that Patricia calls "the Nigerian Princess" contacted Charles and struck up an online communication, convincing him she cared for him. "She said she loved him," Patricia says, "and he fell for it." Since then, her son and daughter have taken control of their father's finances. He was angry about it at first, but he finally agreed. They also convinced him to move to an assisted living facility nearby, now that he is experiencing additional health challenges.

Patricia says their daughter has a better relationship with Charles than she or her son does. She can get him to focus or call him on something he knows isn't right. "It's like he's a rebellious teen and sees her as a parent he needs to con. He's got diabetes and will sneak a hot fudge sundae just to annoy her." Patricia says his living conditions were dismal before their daughter and son stepped in to take over their dad's finances, but she thinks he's in a clean and calm environment now, which makes dealing with him less contentious.

Patricia doesn't know what medications he's receiving, or whether he's being treated for his delusional disorder still, but she says he is compliant with the regimen he's getting from the Veterans' Administration health system. "He's forced to comply, really. The nurse at the assisted living center comes to give him medication, and he just takes it." He's more relaxed because of it, and he seems to welcome the peace it offers.

***

When thinking about her early interactions with mental health professionals during the critical period when Charles was unraveling, Patricia says she was extremely frustrated. Even after he was admitted to the hospital for treatment, she wasn't told what they were doing for him. Confidentiality rules wouldn't allow his doctors to describe his treatment plan to her because Charles hadn't given them permission to do so. Consequently, she was expected to help in his treatment without knowing the specifics of it. It was an impossible situation. She sometimes made requests for modifications but they refused, unless Charles agreed to them. "What kind of arrangement is that? I'm supposed to support the treatment plan, but they wouldn't tell me what the plan was. Instead, he made all the decisions for his care when he wasn't in a condition to make rational decisions."

Patricia suggests she might have been a more effective support for her husband if she hadn't been shut out. "His desires were the priority, which I understand, but as his next of kin, I should have been consulted. They could also have provided some counseling for me and for our kids." A spouse has a unique responsibility toward their partner to seek the best care, make decisions that affect the family, and to support them in ways that other family members can't—children, in particular. Patricia didn't want the children to think they were responsible for their father's breakdown. "It's important the family understands that mental illness is not their fault. It isn't anyone's fault. But no one was there for us. We didn't get any counseling. We rarely talked about it as a family. My kids still don't."

Patricia says she now feels more like a widow than a divorcee. She enjoys the camaraderie of both male and female friends in her senior living apartment complex, which is a new experience for her. "I'd never really had male friends before. I always had girlfriends, but some of the men here are like brothers. It's nice." She says she was tempted to remarry once. She had a serious boyfriend sometime after her divorce, but she couldn't continue in the relationship. "Some part of me is still married," she says. "I still love him," Patricia says. "I made wedding vows, and I take them seriously. My care for him doesn't stop because he became ill. I wish him only the best, but I can't be involved in his everyday life." Frustrated that she was seen as just another divorcee, Patricia wrote a poem to describe her unique feelings toward her marriage and the sadness of how it ended. It began:

> Recently I was reminded
> That most folks see me differently
> Than they see you
> Widows lose their mate
> Divorcees choose their fate.
> But divorce is not a choice I made.
> My husband left his body near me
> When his mind went wherever lost minds go.

Patricia has thought over the years that she'd like to write a book about her experience, because she thinks it might be helpful for another spouse who's experiencing what she did. She doesn't think she can while Charles is still alive, though. "He's not at a point where he could or would read it," she says. "But out of respect for him, I won't. Not while he's alive." She's encouraged her children to tell their stories, but they don't want to. When she asked them if they minded if she was interviewed for this book, they told her, "It's your story, Mom. Tell it."

Samy

About a year after my memoir was published, I got an email from someone named Kaviya who had read my book and wanted to meet me. "I couldn't believe the author of the book I'd just read lives in the same town I do." She got my email address from the local librarian, who had coordinated a book signing for me. Kaviya said she had been diagnosed with mental illness and related deeply to my account of my mother's schizophrenia and our family's response to it.

"I've read every book I can find about mental health and mental illness," Kaviya told me when we met at the library several days later. "When I read the parts of your book taken from your mother's hospital records, I cried." She recognized the treatments described and the incidental descriptions of the psychiatric hospital where my mother was institutionalized. She could see herself in them. Kaviya told me her story of becoming ill many years before and how she had tried to kill herself three times, before she committed to finding help for her condition. "I'm now retired after spending 22 years as a classroom aide in special education." She said she's been doing well the past 20-plus years with appropriate medication and strong family support.

Kaviya's husband Samy was the primary source of support throughout the course of her illness and path to healing. When I reached out to Samy, he was happy to schedule a meeting with me over Zoom. When we met, I first asked him to tell me about Kaviya when they first met, in southern India, where they lived before moving to the US.

"We dated for about 15 minutes before we decided to marry," he says, which makes us both laugh. "We met accidentally through neighbors," he says, "and actually met a second time to confirm our decision." What attracted him to Kaviya was that she was smart, attractive, and friendly. Samy was looking for a partner with a realistic view of life, similar beliefs about the future to his, and a shared value of working hard to achieve goals. "I could see she was also compassionate and caring. She was willing to go out of her way to help others." Despite their brief courtship, their marriage has lasted. They will celebrate their 40th anniversary in 2026. They have two sons, one who lives nearby in Texas. The other lives in New York City.

Samy and Kaviya didn't have any roots or family in the US when they first moved here, which meant they had very little in the way of a support system. "We had friends, though, which can sometimes be better than family." Samy earned his Ph.D. in India but wanted to do research and knew he would have better opportunities in the US. "The US is number one in terms of research. The facilities and opportunities are better here. Many of my colleagues come from other countries for the same reason." But in order to move to the US, Samy had to leave family behind. He was especially sad to leave his mother, who was elderly and alone after he left.

"We didn't need Kaviya's income because I was working," Samy says, of their early married life, "and she was soon taking care of the babies." Samy is a retired medicinal chemist who immigrated to the United States shortly after their marriage, to work at a large Texas university doing research in drug development. "Kaviya began having panic attacks around 1992, and we had no clue what the problem was. Neither of us had any experience in our families with mental illness or anxiety. We just didn't encounter it." At first, they thought her panic attacks were related to some physical illness that could be easily treated, but they eventually realized the problem was not so simply solved. Both sons were young when Kaviya's symptoms began, which complicated their family's life. The boys needed care that, increasingly, Kaviya was unable to provide. Samy had a busy job and found it difficult to manage home and work responsibilities.

"Kaviya had no social network in the US as she had in India, and she was taking care of the children alone. I was working and spent less time with the family than she did." Samy explains that Kaviya has always felt it was her responsibility to be the best at everything because she was terrified of appearing unsuccessful to her parents. Her panic attacks led to depression and feelings of failure, because she wasn't performing as she thought she should. "Things began snowballing, and she was hospitalized in a psychiatric hospital for the first time in 1992. That was a new experience for me. I'd never seen anyone hospitalized for any illness, including mental illness. It was a 180-degree behavior change in my role as her partner."

Samy says he was very confused at first, so he began to research mental illness. "I was feeling lost. I had to educate myself about mental illness. Why it happens. How it happens. It seemed like a never-ending nightmare." Samy had suffered prior disappointments, which are normal, but in his experience, they didn't lead to depression. Instead, he described disappointment as, "falling down, but you always get up. In this case, I started learning that mental illness is something you just can't let go. You keep sliding down. I was a scientist, and this was an area I had to really study." Treatments for mental illness at the time weren't necessarily effective.

The first breakthrough drug was Prozac in the mid-1970s, but many more antipsychotic drugs followed in the next few decades. Kaviya tried almost everything on the market before finding one that worked well for her. Samy estimates she tried 40 to 50 different medications. Some had troubling side effects and some just didn't work. Some increased suicidal thoughts. "She had to try each new drug for four or five weeks to know if it would help, then she had to withdraw to allow her body to flush one drug from her system before trying another one. It took two or three years altogether." That was a difficult time for the family, because sometimes it seemed there was no hope.

"What I learned," Samy says of all this trial and error, "is that drugs can only do so much. She had to want to do the work to find a good treatment. All the time, I was a cheerleader. I was on the sidelines to encourage, but she had to fight." Samy compares mental illness with substance addictions, in that those who are vulnerable to them sometimes don't want to admit they have a problem. Fortunately for Kaviya, she understood that much of her recovery was up to her. Not all individuals with mental illness are this self-aware (Amador et al., 1994). Those suffering from hallucinations as she was are often at the mercy of the "voices" that may tell them to fear those trying to help, or worse, that they should kill themselves.

Individuals like Kaviya with schizoaffective disorder demonstrate symptoms of both schizophrenia and a mood disorder, such as bipolar disorder. An overview of studies by the National Institutes of Health estimates that the lifetime suicide rate among patients with schizophrenia is 10 percent. Suicide accounts for a shorter lifespan, and a decrease of about 10 years in life expectancy for these individuals as a whole. (Sher and Kahn, 2019). In addition, females with schizophrenia are more likely than males to commit suicide, according to the Suicide Prevention Center (2023). Some patients may succeed without family members ever being aware of the voices or illness symptoms that compelled them to take their lives.

"It would have been useful to have a social network during those years," Samy says. "She reached out to family, but they didn't understand mental illness like those who have struggled with it can." Samy says since that time, a niece has had troubling depression, and Kaviya can now be helpful to her sister's family because of her own experiences.

"Treating mental illness is not like bandaging a wound. You can change the bandage, dress the wound, but mental illness is not like other wounds."

Samy, Kaviya, and their sons moved from Texas to a small town in Massachusetts in 1995, where they developed a large network of friends, which was helpful. "The boys would go to a neighbor's home or a neighbor would pick them up from school, at times when Kaviya wasn't able to do it." The family lived in Massachusetts for about 20 years, while the children finished their education.

Because Samy worked in drug development, he interacted with medical facilities and physicians. "I learned a lot through my work, simply by visiting hospitals and medical staff. I learned how challenging it was to identify and treat a mental illness." By the time Kaviya had been hospitalized several times, Samy recognized something troubling in the hospitalization of patients for mental disorders, a situation he noticed in both Massachusetts and Texas. "They housed all mental patients in the same area, regardless of their diagnosis." He noted that some patients have depression or substance addictions, alone or in addition to psychoses. Their behaviors may be totally different because of different diagnoses, yet they are in close proximity to one another. "The science might be the same in some cases," Samy notes, of their treatment, "but the causative agents may be completely different. This was frightening for Kaviya, because she would sometimes fear she would also have the same behaviors as other patients she observed. For drug or alcohol addicts, chemical imbalances due to the abused substance could change their behavior in startling ways, and she feared she would follow the same disease progression others had." It also seemed to Samy that staff members were not as compassionate as they could have been, because of the sometimes bizarre or aggressive behaviors. He worried hospitalization might at times be more harmful than helpful.

Finally, one of Kaviya's doctors did psychological testing and personal interviews with Kaviya and Samy and diagnosed schizoaffective disorder. After intensive discussion with Kaviya, he realized she was experiencing hallucinations, which is a key symptom of both schizophrenia and schizoaffective disorder. This finding helped him prescribe a more specific drug to treat her. Kaviya has been stable for more than 20 years as a result.

One of the most important factors in Kaviya's successful treatment has been her commitment to staying well, according to her husband. "She is determined," Samy says. "She recognizes she will have to take care of herself the rest of her life. She has to manage her symptoms. Circumstances change, and she can get terribly depressed, but she knows how to pull back, how to stop sliding down." In the beginning, she often asked herself, "Why me?" or "What will happen to me?" and "Will I get well?" It's important to know that you *can* get better despite dark times. Support groups could be helpful to both patients and their families, but Samy says the family wasn't offered that kind of support. He emphasizes that drugs alone are not enough. Family support is critical. He and their children have supported Kaviya by helping her restore hope when she feels she's not getting better. When she's exhausted by the emotional drain of being ill, she can collapse and fall back into the deep hole. When her family reminds her that she has gotten better in the past, she is able to regain stability.

Samy advises the professionals who treat persons with mental illness to understand the importance of cooperation between the professional, the patient, and the family. First, the patient has to accept there is a problem and be willing to cooperate with therapy, drugs, exercises, and self-motivation. The family has a role to play in supporting all these things. According to Samy, "Family members benefit from knowledge about what is going on and why it's happening. Sometimes people believe the person with the illness is acting to get attention, or that they don't want to accept failure. They have to understand and be compassionate when their loved one is suffering." He stresses the importance of families educating themselves about the diagnosis and the likely effects of treatments. They also need to be patient when their family member is testing drug regimens or therapies until they find the most effective approach. "It's important to be supportive and not pass judgment. It may be frustrating. I had to work at it. I had to educate myself so I could work with the doctors to help with decision making."

***

Kaviya's illness has been stressful for the whole family. Their children were young while she was unable to care for them as well as she would have liked. Samy was often stressed by worry over his work and taking care of his family. He traveled frequently, often being away from home for days or a week at a time. He credits their friends and neighbors in Massachusetts with helping to keep the children safe and healthy. Kaviya attempted suicide twice while their sons were in middle school. Each time, she was hospitalized in a psychiatric hospital and given Electroconvulsive Therapy (ECT), which provided little long-term relief. Things improved in the mid-1990s, but there was another suicide attempt in 2001 before a helpful drug and therapy regimen was finally found.

"I urged Kaviya, once she was more stable, to get involved with family activities. Because of the drugs, she could sometimes be like a zombie and had no clue what was going on." Those side effects eventually eased, fortunately. To engage with their children and their friends, she was encouraged to volunteer at the kids' school, where she could spend more time with children, including her own. Volunteering required her to keep a structured schedule, which was also helpful. "Once she started spending time at the school, the more structured environment helped her get her confidence back. She'd been convinced she was unfit for normal living," but being useful at the school lifted her spirits. Samy says they took it one day at a time, and slowly things got better.

Once their sons were grown and had completed college, Samy and Kaviya decided to move to a warmer climate. Their sons were present through some very distressing times. They also became educated about their mother's illness and stood steadfastly in support of her, according to their father. "However, the boys have their own lives, and I was thinking of retirement." The couple chose to move back to Texas in 2017, where one son now lives. "We never intended to stay in Massachusetts permanently. It was too cold." Samy's plans to retire were upended, though, when his company asked him to stay on and work remotely in customer support. He agreed to continue working from home but finally retired completely in 2023.

***

Despite some sadness at leaving family in India many years ago, Samy is grateful for their life here. He had no experience with mental illness in his earlier life and isn't sure what mental health support was available in India for those who needed it, and he recognizes the situation may be quite different now. He's satisfied with the mental health support they've received in the US. At the same time, he insists inner strength is the most important ingredient for successful coping. "I have never lost hope, even when Kaviya tried to kill herself, even when she was unconscious in the hospital. You have to trust in yourself. I always tell my children to think of tomorrow. Things will get better. They already have a better situation than many others."

Remaining hopeful doesn't mean that caring for a family member struggling with a mental illness is easy. "Immediate family members—in our case a spouse and children—suffer silently. Someone needs to reach them. Our 16-year-old niece has mental health issues and is often in the hospital. A chaplain works with her, but the family is also supported spiritually and emotionally. This gives her family the strength to care for her. Understanding the disorder is the number one issue." Samy says he hasn't really found this kind of support for himself. However, he and their sons encourage Kaviya by standing by her always and reminding her that she has the power to keep herself healthy. He says his messages to her are, "You've been here before. You can do it. This is not permanent. This is not forever. You will get through it."

As a result of her strong family support, Kaviya is committed to being an example to others. Samy estimates that she has read at least a thousand books about mental illness. She finds hope in each of the stories. She wants her story to provide hope to others as well. She and Samy both realize that the stigma of mental illness keeps many from speaking up, and they agree it shouldn't be that way.

After the couple returned to Texas, she continued to work as a classroom aide for special education students, work that helped her feel she was making a difference. She retired when her husband did so that they could enjoy traveling together. According to Samy, when they travel, they freely express their knowledge about mental illness and describe how they've been able to find health and hope in spite of it. "Mental illness is nothing to be ashamed of. People should be proud to emerge from it successfully."

Referring to a common saying from India when he was a child, Samy compares a person with a mental illness to a pancake. He explains. "You know how every pancake has little bubbles, popping air pockets? No matter who makes the pancakes, they're full of tiny holes and every hole has the same thing inside." No pancake is perfect or the same as every other pancake. Each pancake tastes wonderful, no matter where the holes appear. I appreciate the idea that each pancake is different, with different holes in different places, just as people are all different: made of the same materials but demonstrating equally wonderful shapes and sizes. This is a valuable message.

However, I am most impressed by Samy's enthusiastic role as a cheerleader for Kaviya. I'm not sure she would be as healthy as she is today without his ever-present support and that of their sons. Who among us wouldn't appreciate a cheerleader like that?

Celeste

"Elaine has experienced many traumas in her life," her partner Celeste tells me. "Even as a teen she faced emotional violence and sexual abuse. She continues to face racial trauma." As a Black queer woman, Elaine has been the target of multiple sources of trauma. According to Celeste, these traumas are the likely source of her clinical depression and anxiety disorder. She also thinks the chronic and debilitating back pain Elaine suffers from is related to trauma. "Some days, the pain is so bad, she can't leave the bed. She may sit in a chair for a time, but then it becomes too painful just to sit." Elaine and Celeste, who is a native of Togo but spent 20 years in France before moving to the UK, have been together for more than a year.

Elaine was a teacher of religious studies for six years in a secondary school but is now pursuing an advanced degree in research and hopes to eventually enroll in a local university PhD program related to the intersection of racism and religious studies. As a teacher, she sponsored a club for Black students to explore this intersection, something she's passionate about. "It's a heavy topic," Celeste says. "Elaine has experienced a lot of racism and abuse personally, and while the routine of work helps her, dealing with those topics in her work adds to her ill health. When she's not at work, her defenses come down, and that's when she's left to deal with the history of abuse." Celeste says Elaine's work induces reexperiencing racism and mental trauma, which then affects her relationships with her coworkers and others. But Celeste believes that focusing on the traumas that affected her personally through her work and her study also helps her process them.

Despite Elaine's illnesses, she manages to function well enough. "Work comes first. Everything comes after work, including her relationships. In her work, she is so focused that she doesn't think about her anxiety or depression. Her pain is a reminder of her conditions, however. Somehow, she keeps it all together," Celeste says. "She works very hard not to demonstrate to her colleagues that she's in pain, but it takes a toll on her. When she comes home from work or a day of study, she is completely exhausted and in severe pain. The pain is generally in her back and radiates to her feet." Celeste says it's important to Elaine never to miss a day of work, no matter how much pain she is in. Her perception is that it will diminish her standing among her peers if she succumbs to the pain. "She's very intelligent and good at her job, but she feels she has to continually prove it."

Elaine's teaching provided structure for her and allowed her a place to focus, which was useful but draining. Transitioning to doing research instead of teaching has been challenging because of the change in her routine. It's now up to Elaine to schedule her coursework. "As a teacher, she had to go to work at a certain time, and so on. Her notion of time is very different now." The transition has exacerbated her pain. "She can't sleep well because she has night terrors with intrusive thoughts that disrupt her sleep. She still functions, but she has to dig and dig for the strength—not every day, but frequently. For example, her chronic pain issues make it even more difficult to have a seat in the university when she has lessons. It's hard for her to sit comfortably because of the back pain, but she has to go through a whole process at the school and say 'I have chronic pain', and she doesn't want to be labeled as disabled or to think of herself as disabled." Celeste says she would have to push to get a more comfortable chair. They're available, but if Elaine wants one, she will have to carry the chair to her class herself, which is too hard for her. The university isn't very accommodating, according to Celeste, and Elaine tries to soldier through. It seems the price of keeping things together manifests itself in greater anxiety and depression, however.

"She's very much in her own head much of the time, which can be isolating," Celeste says. "It isn't always possible to know what she's thinking. She is sometimes detached, but her anxiety comes across in our everyday interactions. Her behavior depends on her perceptions and is driven by the anxiety. She is always thinking about the worst-case scenarios and assuming a lot about every situation. She's anxious that something bad will happen, or that she did something wrong, or that she's going to be abandoned or shut out." Celeste believes Elaine feels threatened as a result of past abuse where her boundaries were violated. When she's triggered or overwhelmed by events that Celeste may not be aware of, she shuts down. Even seemingly normal interactions can trigger her. "Sometimes, it's hard for me to reach her."

Although she can become very distant at times, Celeste says Elaine has a deep fear of being left behind. The couple spend significant time together, and when they're not together, Elaine's depression sometimes makes it hard to get through her days without anxiety. She will say she has to do this one small thing or that *necessary* thing won't happen, which exacerbates her anxiety. She's often not emotionally capable of tackling the day. It can be a vicious cycle. "When the depression hits, she isolates herself and doesn't go out. Or she will turn to comfort eating, which isn't healthy either."

***

Celeste is often frustrated by Elaine's tendency to distance herself when she's struggling. "She doesn't have other friends and doesn't go out. I encourage it, but she just doesn't. I know she's had suicidal thoughts in the past, which worries me, but they seem to have decreased. It's still a fleeting thought." Celeste, on the other hand, makes a point of going out with friends occasionally and thinks it helps her maintain balance. She sees her role as a support person for Elaine in listening and understanding without judgment. "I can be physically present to relieve her pain. I can carry things for her that are difficult for her to carry. I can reassure her when she's anxious. I can tell her, 'Everything's okay,' or help her talk through what she's anxious about and help her gain a new perspective."

Celeste says talking through things helps Elaine reframe her perceptions. "Sometimes when it comes to our relationship, I have to reassure her that we're all good. I have to say, 'that's not what I said' or 'that's not what I meant.' It's a matter of reframing." However, whenever Elaine shuts Celeste out, it's difficult. "She just disappears emotionally sometimes and won't respond anymore. That's been a very difficult thing for me to deal with in the relationship, but I'm doing better." Celeste says they're both working on navigating the emotional and physical barriers Elaine constructs. "I know I do sometimes act as her therapist, and that's not my role, but I think in this case it's needed. I try to help her see things differently when it comes to work and when it comes to her mental health." Celeste reminds Elaine to stick to her schedule to help her stay focused. At other times, Celeste may offer to take care of details when Elaine is overwhelmed.

Celeste says Elaine is also neurodivergent, which can make planning things challenging for her. Providing a healthy structure to her is helpful. "For instance, going to the gym is something that really helps her mental health, but she may plan to do something else instead, and then not go to the gym. Then she feels bad and she'll start eating. I'll say, 'What are you doing? Are you comfort eating?' to help her see she's not coping well." Celeste says she will remind Elaine how much better she feels when she goes to the gym and encourages her to go. She tries to keep her accountable for the strategies that help her feel better. When she doesn't follow through, Elaine can spiral down to feeling worse. Celeste will suggest to Elaine that when she feels depressed, there are specific constructive things she can do to help her mood or disposition. They talk it through together.

"When Elaine travels for work, I can help her plan for the trip. I can arrange for accommodations or suggest a bag that's easier for her to manage." In addition, when they go somewhere together, Celeste helps by making sure Elaine is comfortable in their environment. Celeste helps her create and keep a schedule. She tells Elaine it's easier to deal with things that bother her if she talks about them and avoids holding things in so that they become negative.

***

Elaine does not take medication for her depression or anxiety, but she does take painkillers for her pain. "They're not all that effective, in my opinion," Celeste says. "She still has pain, and it can be complicated to time when she takes the medication. The stress of timing adds to her anxiety." Sometimes the pain is intense and it's been difficult for Elaine to grapple with the fact that the pain may be a permanent, everyday part of her life.

Elaine has consulted a psychologist, a chiropractor, a physical therapist, and a deep tissue masseuse at various times for her mental and physical health issues. She now sees a psychologist regularly for talk therapy. She's worked with the same therapist for several years and feels comfortable with her. Celeste isn't sure what interactions Elaine has had with the National Health Service, but thinks she has a fear of navigating complicated systems for accessing services or making appointments. Celeste doubts she has used it and thinks Elaine's inability to access resources could also contribute to her anxiety.

"I go to therapy myself," Celeste says. "It gives me a space to share how I feel and the difficulties I have caring for Elaine and helps me center myself. It's sometimes hard to find space for me in our relationship. Her problems take a lot of my energy—she's not being difficult on purpose—but it's draining. It's hard to say how I feel because she may not take it well. I'm afraid it will trigger her anxiety. I have to wait until she's in a place where she can receive what I have to say."

For her own sake, Celeste has to create a life outside the relationship. "I do things just for me," Celeste says. "I meet with friends to hike or to just do things without Elaine. It helps me recenter and recharge. I have my own mental health issues, but not to the same extent. It's important for me to find time for myself, find energy for myself, so I can deal with my own life. I'm conscious about taking care of myself. I tend to pour into others, and I'm learning to pour into myself as well." She believes it's good for her to do some things that don't center Elaine.

Celeste has never met Elaine's therapist but believes Elaine has a good rapport with the therapist. "Elaine's comfortable with her. On that count, she goes—I never have to remind her to see her therapist." Celeste says she worries she's too invested in Elaine's well-being. She thinks they need to draw the line between what is hers to do and what is Elaine's to do and to learn. They need to work out what responsibilities they each need to account for in their relationship. "We've discussed couples therapy and we hope to do that at some point in the future." One of Elaine's fears is becoming too dependent on Celeste. "I understand, but there are times it's appropriate to depend on other people, especially with the constant pain." Elaine just doesn't seem able to reach out for help. Celeste tries to explain it's not the same thing as dependency. This is where Elaine expanding her community beyond colleagues and Celeste could be an asset. "Community is important," Celeste says. "I keep encouraging her to cultivate community and friendship. I suggest we go into spaces with other people, to go to the symphony or something. However, I don't think she's ready for that. She does have a few friends, but her isolation game is very strong. She's very secretive and doesn't share much. She has friends who don't know about her life really." Group support for her chronic pain might be useful, but it's difficult for Elaine to open up about it. "I think it would help her see how others deal with similar situations and learn how they cope with them, but I don't think she would go."

Even if Elaine were interested in participating in community mental health resources, Celeste doesn't think support systems are well known. "Neither of us knows how or where to find them." She says Elaine's employer or university might supply some mental health support, but it's indirect and not adequate. At the university, what they do offer is simply a center where students can go, or where they occasionally plan an activity students can attend. Celeste doesn't see that a center is useful for people with mental health conditions, because they don't want to draw attention to themselves in a public setting.

Instead, Celeste says she stretches out her hand to Elaine and hopes she will take it and accompany her to places where she could benefit from community. "Elaine would not take advantage of employer-provided services, I don't think." A better alternative would be a space structured for Black people or queer people," according to Celeste. "That intersection is important. If you feel like you're not represented, it would be hard to go to a place where you have to explain yourself." Celeste believes it would be important to understand Elaine's perspective as a Black queer woman, as well as her experiences with racism, her experiences at work, or in life. Because of past abuses related to her identity, Elaine fears future possible incidents of racism and homophobia. "Her identity as a Black queer woman impacts her impression of herself, and then her depression and anxiety. It's all linked. It's not just depression; it's what created the depression. It's very personal, and it's also structures in society that impact her mental health and how she goes through life." Celeste says it would be ideal to have spaces where all who participate can be treated equally and where appropriately trained care workers understand the intersection of identities and how that impacts mental health.

***

Recently, Elaine traveled for her work and stayed in a hotel. "Her bed was very uncomfortable, and the challenge of having to advocate for herself, to say, 'I need another bed. The one in my room is uncomfortable' was difficult. They changed it once, but it was still uncomfortable. The clerk at the front desk was annoyed. When the wife of a colleague came to the desk, the behavior changed. He was more accommodating. All those things add to her pain." Celeste says every aspect of Elaine's life is impacted by her mental state and her physical pain, but complicated by the intersection of her various identities.

According to Celeste, structural racism can also make one-on-one therapy difficult. Even after the years Elaine has been working with her current therapist, who is white, Celeste knows Elaine sometimes has to educate the therapist on racism and the Black perspective. They've worked together for a long time, and Elaine is comfortable with her, so she seems satisfied. "My therapist is Black, because I didn't want to have to do that kind of training. Care workers need to understand how racism and gender identity impact their patients." Celeste went on to emphasize the importance of having a professional caregiver recognize the effects of being Black and queer. Celeste says she hasn't even come out to her parents, so she knows it's a difficult topic to approach. "Therapy, for me, is a place where I can be vulnerable without masking, without hiding part of myself. Where I don't have to risk racism, even when it's not intentional."

Celeste considers herself an advocate for Elaine, but she thinks one way to more effectively advocate for Elaine's health is to advocate for her own. "When I realized I needed therapy, I found a therapist. It's easy to get lost in caring for the people we love, because we want them to be happy. But we need to take time for ourselves so we can continue to be a good support system for them." She says another vital ingredient in a support system is patience. Mental illness does not resolve easily or quickly.

Celeste says she's shocked at the lack of public services in the UK, compared to those in France, where she spent two decades. "We seem to be living in an era where everything is privatized, at least in the UK. And the Prime Minister talks about wanting to remove aid for disabled citizens. It's irritating." She doesn't hold out much hope for immediate improvement but would like to see better support for people with mental illness. She thinks taxes should provide mental health and healthcare support services for those who are disabled or who can't provide for themselves. "Mental illness is not like cancer, for instance, where you can see it on a film or a scan." Celeste thinks it's unfortunate that there is a tendency to dismiss mental health as unimportant. However, the COVID-19 pandemic showed us how important it is, she says, and it will get more complicated.

"I call Elaine a 'Warrior' because despite everything she's been through, she's still here. She's still fighting. She's put in a lot of effort to be in a relationship and to get better. I know it's not easy in a society not made for her."

6
Lessons for policymakers

Introduction

It was an incredible honor to be trusted with the stories of the individuals featured in the previous chapters. Dealing with a family member's mental illness is painful and disruptive. In addition, the public's bias against individuals whose behavior differs from social "norms" contributes to a persistent stigma regarding mental illnesses. The stigma makes it difficult to talk openly about having family members with mental health conditions. I am grateful for the courage of these parents, children, siblings, and partners who advocate for their loved ones despite the challenges of an often inadequate mental health care system and a society that fears or ostracizes them. I also appreciate their honesty in exposing the gaps in services they encountered when seeking appropriate care for their relatives. Their stories demonstrate that families face several common complications within mental health systems that have failed them or that have prevented them from finding the help their loved one needs. On the other hand, each family experiences unique challenges, due to disorder characteristics and symptoms, family dynamics, or geographic locations.

Many of the obstacles families face could be overcome if family members were invited to participate in their loved one's care. I propose that it isn't possible to successfully treat a patient or client with mental illness in isolation from their family system. Treatment success is more likely assured when mental health practitioners encourage participation from the parents, siblings, or partners—and in some cases, children—of those they serve.

Several mental health studies support this conclusion. While most studies confirm the positive effects of family involvement (FI) in a patient's care, a few recommend caution in cases of unhealthy family dynamics, and both will be referenced here. However, research studies can only go so far in informing best practices. Real people in real situations who love someone with mental illness and struggle to help them have stories to tell. Those stories deserve the attention of mental health professionals. Practitioners and family members can and should become partners, whenever possible, in providing the optimal care for individuals with mental illness.

In the following sections, I present some obstacles family members shared with me in helping their loved ones receive appropriate treatment, selected research study results, recommendations for improvements in care, and a brief look toward the future.

Obstacles to appropriate diagnosis and treatment

The National Alliance on Mental Illness (NAMI) provides state-by-state statistics on mental health. Their data show information about how many people in the state have mental health conditions, how many are uninsured, how many have few or no mental health professionals near them, suicide rates and more. In many states, the number of mental health professionals at all levels is dangerously low. For example, in Texas, where I live, more than 15 million citizens—almost 49% of Texans—live in communities without enough providers, and 18.4% of Texas residents have no health insurance (NAMI, 2021), compared to 8% of Americans nationwide who are without health insurance. This means Texas is near last in that measure. If a family is fortunate enough to locate services in their community but has no insurance, they may not be able to afford them. For Margo, who found the National Health Service in the UK woefully inadequate, the only option was to pay privately for care. This is the case for too many patients.

Depending on where they live, families have a patchwork of insurance obstacles to navigate. This, despite a national law requiring the same access to mental health care as to physical health care. Insurer openness to approving care varies a good bit state to state. In some states, there are laws that govern what criteria the insurer must use in deciding whether to cover mental health treatment, and the state monitors insurers to guarantee they apply those criteria. Criteria established by professional mental health societies are highly recommended as a standard, but many states do not require that insurers use them. On the other hand, some states require only that insurers adhere to vague criteria that are not evidence-based. In the absence of stringent requirements, insurers set their own standards, which can be unsound in terms of accepted mental health practice. They may also severely limit physician-recommended treatments so that what they *do* approve is far from adequate.

Without oversight, insurers may not share how their standards for coverage are derived at all. Some review private records of patient-provider sessions before choosing whether to approve treatment, creating confidentiality concerns. Complicating matters further, even when well-designed state mandates exist, insurers often don't follow them and states fail to enforce them (Waldman and Miller, 2024). It's no surprise that families and their loved ones are frustrated.

Further frustrating a family's efforts are restraints imposed by the Health Insurance Portability and Accountability Act (HIPAA). Enacted in 1996, HIPAA ensures portability of an individual's insurance in circumstances such as a change in employment. It also protects the privacy of health information (US Dept. of Health and Human Services, 2025). While features of the law are certainly beneficial, it has potential drawbacks—it often prevents family members of those with Serious Mental Illness (SMI) from participating in their relatives' medical care, including requesting evaluation for psychiatric conditions. SMI is a term used by mental health professionals to describe disorders that significantly impair a person's ability to function in daily life. Even when this level of disability exists, parents of adult children are shut out of decision-making unless their child expressly authorizes it. Many adult patients with schizophrenia or bipolar disorder dispute their diagnosis. They may refuse evaluation or treatment. In those cases, a parent can't assist in securing appropriate care for them.

Even adult patients who concur with an SMI diagnosis often demand the freedom to make independent medical decisions and refuse a relative's input. Unfortunately, their decisions may be heavily influenced by disordered thinking, delusions, or auditory hallucinations. As a result, interactions with mental health professionals are less effective, at best, and potentially dangerous at worst. Inaccurate information about symptomatology may preclude precise or appropriate treatment.

Another frustration voiced by the family members I interviewed was the lack of communication between themselves and their loved ones' service providers. While a few were consulted for input, as Greg was once for his partner and Margaret still is for her sister Barb, most were not. A few didn't even know who provided care for their relative. This can be a serious problem when the loved one is diagnosed with psychosis and is ineffectively medicated or chooses not to adhere to a treatment schedule.

Many patients are unable to accurately report their symptoms or circumstances, as Sylvia found in the case of her brother Doug. In many cases, family members are better equipped to provide it. Studies by Hestmark, et al. (2023) and Ong, Fernandez, and Lim (2021) demonstrated that involving family members in treatment generally leads to a better outcome for the diagnosed individual. An Iranian study by Dehbozorgi, et al. (2022), as well as the Hestmark et al. study mentioned above (2023) caution that family involvement (FI) can be unhelpful in the case of unhealthy family dynamics, but with that caveat in mind, all studies find that FI is desirable when family members are able to contribute positively to their loved one's care.

What the research says

The most positive effects of family involvement are seen in cases of adolescent mental illness. Family therapy, specifically single-session therapy (one issue, one goal) proves to be the most effective model in the treatment of youth diagnosed with schizophrenia, depression, ADHD, anxiety, and anorexia (Goodman, D. and Happell, B, 2006). Ann and her daughter Olivia demonstrate the effectiveness of working together as a family to manage Olivia's symptoms.

Peer education programs appear to be highly effective for family members as well. NAMI provides classes to family members, notably the Family-to-Family peer support class that Sarah taught. This program educates family members about serious mental illnesses and provides resources for obtaining proper treatment. Being prepared to deal with their relative's disease progression or hearing strategies shared by other families in this way is reassuring. Perhaps the greatest benefit is that class members feel supported when they discover others have experienced similar challenges and have dealt successfully with them. Sharing each other's stories in this setting strengthens the family system and enables them to more effectively help their loved one adhere to treatment (Schiffman et al., 2015).

D. J. Jaffe, author of *Insane Consequences: How the Mental Health Industry Fails the Mentally Ill* and director of Mental Illness Policy Org stresses the distinction between mental health conditions and serious mental illness. In his opinion, lumping them together has led to failure to address either one effectively. He thinks those with SMI are ignored when drafting mental health policy for the aggregate. For instance, while it is true that those with a diagnosed mental health condition are more likely to be victims of crime than perpetrators (see 1. Introduction), untreated individuals with SMI are more violent on average than other individuals (Jaffe, 2017 pp. 31 – 33). They often end up incarcerated as a result, which he sees as simply a substitute for the asylum model of caring for the mentally ill. Like many of those interviewed for this book, he is frustrated by the barriers relatives encounter when attempting to intervene in a loved one's mental health crisis because the criteria require intent to commit violence, if not actual violent acts before intervention is possible. He insists policy should focus on *preventing* violence, not simply reacting to it, as is the norm for current policy (Jaffe, 2017, p. 34). Jaffe concludes that FI improves outcomes for patients with SMI in addition to saving costs (Jaffe, 2017, p. 76). He is also a strong advocate for HIPAA reform.

Concurring with the suggestion that FI improves outcomes, a 2004 meta-analysis of 25 intervention studies found that relapse and rehospitalization rates for schizophrenia treatment were reduced when family members were involved in treatment. Some types of intervention studied included psychoeducational groups, educational lectures for relatives, and group therapy for families, all of which can be considered "psychoeducation."When psychosocial support is provided to the patient and family in tandem, outcome is more positive than medication-only treatment. The article states that despite the positive results, practitioners rarely involve a patient's family in treatment (Pitschel-Walz, et al., 2004).

A more recent study demonstrates benefits of FI in patient treatment in four areas: family psychoeducation regarding the framework, reduction of conflict or stress, triadic understanding (between family member, diagnosed individual, and provider), and a sense of all involved being on the same team (Hestmark et al., 2023). These are considered the primary effects. The same study identified a few drawbacks to FI, which they found less frequently than the benefits: difficulty of some family members in following the framework, family over-involvement, and relatives who may be negative influences. Assuming these potential pitfalls can be avoided, the authors conclude FI should be considered (Hestmark et al., 2023).

A 2021 article in the *Singapore Journal of Medicine* promotes family engagement in managing patients with mental illness (Ong, Fernandez, and Lim, 2021). In particular, the authors recommend psychoeducation, support of individual family needs, and family assessment or therapy. They also list international organizations that support family involvement, including the World Psychiatric Association and the World Health Organization Mental Health Action Plan (Ong, Fernandez, and Lim, 2021).

While FI is encouraged, there are also barriers to successful FI. One study in Iran noted four categories of barriers—two of them related to limitations of individual family situations or specific treatment factors (Dehbozorgi et al., 2022). The illness involved may also create specific challenges that FI doesn't effectively address, or the stigma surrounding mental illness is too great for families to desire involvement. While cultural factors in Iran likely differ from those in other countries, these concerns are valid and worth investigating.

These research references are not intended to be exhaustive, but rather illustrative of the factors to consider when inviting family members to contribute to their loved one's care. As Sarah told me when describing her frustration with her and John's inability to participate in Ryan's treatment decisions, particularly when treatment fails. "We're the only people there to pick up the pieces." If they were active members of Ryan's care team, everyone would likely benefit.

Recommendations

The following recommendations incorporate suggestions from family members as well as research conclusions about improving mental health services to families. Mental health professionals often have greater power to revise policy than do family members, but many changes are enhanced through joint advocacy by family members and professionals. Heartfelt personal stories about family traumas are often more compelling to lawmakers than purely professional opinions. When personal stories and professional opinions converge to promote revised mental health policies, legislators are more likely to act (Fadlallah et al., 2019). Five areas in which policy changes would make a difference for families are listed below, along with specific suggestions.

1. HIPAA reform

Several people interviewed suggested that the criteria for intervention when a family member is experiencing a mental health crisis are too narrow to allow involuntary hospitalization or other intervention. If Beth and her husband had been able to insist on mental health evaluation and treatment, as they attempted to do while their son was detained in jail, he might still be alive. Their inability to intervene due to HIPAA restrictions may have contributed to his disappearance and presumed death. D. J. Jaffe recommends several reforms to HIPAA law that make common sense exceptions in cases like this one. His suggestions would protect patients from undue infringement on their privacy rights while allowing families the ability to make sensible decisions for optimum care (Jaffe, 2017, pp. 267–268).

- Extend exemptions in HIPAA law that exist to benefit insurance companies to family members. Existing exemptions allow insurance companies to access health records when making coverage decisions.

- Exclude those who have exhibited dangerous behavior due to mental illness in the past from HIPAA protections for a limited time after hospitalization to allow for involuntary interventions when essential to avoid additional risky behavior.

- Allow physicians to disclose medical information to family members for patients who lack sufficient mental capacity to make care decisions, who are seriously mentally ill, or who have been incarcerated due to mental illness.

- Require physicians to solicit relevant patient information from trusted and reliable family members, rather than merely allowing it.

- Rather than requiring patient consent before disclosure of records, require only that a "good faith effort" has been made to obtain consent.

- Insulate physicians from liability for good-faith efforts to disclose information from a trusted and reliable source, when they believe it is in the best interest of their patients.

2. Education and support

Several decades ago, beginning in the 1960s and 1970s, care of those with mental illness shifted from an institutional model to a community model of mental health care. Across the US, mental hospitals were purged of long-term residents, leaving family members unprepared and ill-equipped for the greater responsibility of care for their loved ones. Though some of the motivation for these changes resulted from advancements in psychotropic drug therapy or reports of abuses at these facilities, financial concerns drove many changes. Operating state psychiatric hospitals is expensive. Communities that were able to created short-term residency facilities or mental health clinics to serve their residents. Not all communities have enough resources to provide adequate services, however. Many provide nothing at all. Amy has found that telling her story in community training sessions for first responders helps them understand the nature of SMI and deal more effectively with individuals in mental health crises. National organizations like NAMI have stepped up in many areas to provide services to both patients and families, and other community groups have initiated creative and supportive programs for their residents. Some recommendations for community health services regarding education and support include:

- Invite family members of those diagnosed with mental illness to participate in community training events for law enforcement, fire departments, emergency medical personnel, and others who encounter individuals in crisis.
- Conduct classes for family members that describe SMIs, symptoms, and likely disease progression to prepare them adequately to care for a loved one with mental illness.
- Provide a resource directory of local physicians, medical professionals, or mental health networks and assist families in accessing them.
- Encourage programs for self-care, such as physical exercise, yoga, meditation, individual counseling, EMDR, retreats,

support groups, journaling workshops, social outings with friends, arts and crafts activities, etc.

• Recommend peer support groups, in which all participants can safely share their experiences and challenges.

• Provide patients and families with access to stories of others who struggle with mental illness. This collection is one example.

3. Family involvement

Restraints posed by HIPAA law are not the only impediments to incorporating family members' concerns when treating a patient with SMI. Reforms in the law would make family involvement simpler and improve a patient's chances of successful treatment. However, unless a provider recognizes the value of consultation with family members, they are not motivated to seek it. For families who provide physical support for a relative (housing, food, transportation, etc.), being shut out of symptom management is extremely frustrating. Sarah and John, for instance, found it impossible for their son to live with them because of his behavior and their inability to participate in treatment, and they have no control over his current living conditions. For partners who are shut out of care decisions, having a partner with SMI who lives in the home with them and minor children may prove untenable, as Patricia discovered.

When family members are allowed access to their loved one's mental health care team, they are better able to provide an environment that works for all family members. Some suggestions for providers to include family members in treatment include:

• Consult with family members during the initial assessment of a patient to determine the validity of the patient's claims of symptoms. Solicit input from family about how a patient's behaviors are perceived and how they affect those living in the home with them.

- Meet with the patient and family members together on a periodic basis (quarterly or semi-annually, for instance) to check on the status of the patient's symptoms over time. Much can be learned from family members about observed changes in patient behavior that cannot be learned from the patient alone.
- Consider visiting a patient in their home to determine what challenges to the patient, if any, exist in the home. Assess family dynamics to determine how best to utilize family members as treatment allies.
- Recommend family therapy on an ongoing, regular basis for families to communicate with each other in a safe, but controlled environment.

4. Safety

Although Sylvia and her brother Richard have been fortunate in finding a suitable group home setting for their brother, they first experienced some hair-raising experiences with callous or unqualified caregivers who pocketed his funds and provided less than adequate care. One caregiver abused several family members. Others have discovered issues that affect the safety of the family or the diagnosed individual. Possible remedies include:

- Advocate for adequate oversight of caregivers in in-home care or group homes for those with mental illness diagnoses. Promote state oversight of caregivers, with drop-in, unannounced visits, as are routinely done for childcare centers.
- Advocate for a group-home concept in communities where such a situation is not available. State support and oversight are critical.

- Advocate for stringent gun restrictions for those who have a history of SMI, combined with a history of violent behaviors or suicidal ideation.
- Monitor the well-being of minor children in the sole care of a parent with mental illness who has a history of risky or violent behavior. Enlist trusted and reliable family members to participate in such monitoring.

5. Stigma

Several people interviewed suggested that mental health professionals have an obligation to eliminate the current stigma surrounding mental illness. They also have a more public platform from which to advocate change than families do. Open public dialogue about symptoms and treatment would do much to offset society's fears when confronted with diagnosed individuals. As Samy discovered, talking openly about Kaviya's struggle frees them from much of the stigma associated with her illness. Other suggestions for professionals follow.

- Make it clear to patients and families that SMI is no one's fault. Stress that mental illness is an illness like any other disease and should receive the same level of attention.
- Participate in public forums in which accurate information is disseminated about SMI, its symptoms and treatment.
- Participate in training for first responders and provide credible information about how to approach someone having a mental health crisis from a professional perspective.

What does the future hold?

Research into the etiology and treatment of mental illness has been robust in the past several decades. Pharmacological research has succeeded in discovering a host of drugs to successfully manage symptoms of SMI, and many have been lifesaving for those who need them. In addition, research into methods such as psychotherapy, EMDR, or Cognitive Behavioral Therapy (CBT) helps many people manage their disease. Just as important is research into the causes of mental illness. Understanding them might yield preventive strategies.

There are no easy answers or one-size-fits-all treatments. It is likely that each person with SMI has a unique combination of contributing factors, from individual biochemistry and genetics to brain structure or environment. So far, there have been no dramatic discoveries of a "schizophrenia gene," for instance, though genetics is one vigorous avenue of research. Research has determined there are genetic links to many mental illnesses, but there is not yet a definitive answer to why some persons with the same genetic makeup develop a disease but their identical twin does not. Environmental or experiential factors are likely involved, but which ones? How are they avoided?

Mental illness research is complicated, though one ongoing study proposes we should not overlook simple solutions. For instance, Dr. Robert Freedman suggests that choline supplements given to pregnant women may prevent schizophrenia development in their offspring. Choline is essential to fetal brain development (Zhaori, 2020). The good news is that choline has no adverse side effects, so ingesting supplements is no danger to a pregnant woman or her fetus. The bad news is that it takes decades for the children of mothers in the clinical trial to become adults and to assess the success of the supplements. Fortunately, this is not Freedman's only schizophrenia study. As is true of many other research scientists, his research includes several approaches to the same disease.

Other research efforts are varied and widespread. In the US, the National Institute of Mental Health and the National Alliance on Mental Illness, among several other national organizations conduct or fund extensive research into mental illness. The World Health Organization does international research, and in the UK, Mental Health Research and the National Institute for Health and Care Research contribute to psychiatric data. Many other studies are funded by grants and carried out by faculty at universities or specialists at scientific organizations around the world who provide vital information about mental illness causes and treatment. Each study relies on the intuition of a particular scientist and their commitment to a hypothesis about mental illness that motivates them to undergo research. It would not be possible to catalog each of them here. It is also worth noting that this depth of research only occurs when those who control the grant money are willing to invest in it. That cannot be ensured, as administrations change and opinions differ on what avenues of research to pursue.

Certified mental health professionals engage in continuing education, which includes subscribing to scholarly journals such as those referenced here and attending conferences at which research findings are presented. However, stories of individuals personally affected by the ravages of mental illness are also an important part of a practitioner's education. I propose that mental health professionals actively seek out such stories and learn from families' experiences.

Appendix I

Interview questions

Every person's story is unique, so the following questions provide only a framework for a discussion about how mental illness has affected you and your loved one. Some questions may not apply, but others may arise as we talk that help you better communicate your experiences. Please consider what follows in advance of our interview.

1. What condition or diagnosis does/did your loved one live with? How old was he/she at diagnosis or onset?

2. Describe your relationship with your loved one prior to diagnosis and after. How did it change? How has it affected your relationships with other family members or friends?

3. Compare and contrast your home life before and after your loved one's diagnosis.

4. What efforts have you made, or did you make, to help your loved one receive an accurate diagnosis and effective treatment? What was the result?

5. Can you describe your loved one before he/she was affected by the illness? How has she/he changed since the illness developed?

6. How would you describe the difficulties of living with a mental illness?

7. What resources have been helpful to you or to your loved one?

8. Has finding medical or psychiatric resources in your community been challenging? Why or why not?

9. What tools or strategies have helped you cope with the stress of supporting someone with mental illness?

10. Do you consider yourself an advocate for mental health for your loved one and/or others who live with mental illness? In what ways?

11. What else would you like others to know about your loved one? About you or your family?

12. What advice could you share with another person dealing with a mentally ill family member?

13. Where have you found support for yourself, your loved one, or other family members as you navigate the issues mental illness has forced you to confront?

14. What suggestions do you have for mental health policy-makers to more effectively assist families in dealing with mental illness? What resources should be made available?

Appendix II

Mental health conditions

Each of the following conditions appears in at least one family story included in this book. Brief descriptions of the illness and an overview of symptoms are included here. The information in this section is summarized from much more extensive data on the NAMI website page "Mental Health Conditions" (National Association on Mental Illness). The stories presented here and the NAMI website demonstrate that individuals diagnosed with these conditions generally find talk therapy, individual counseling, or behavioral therapy beneficial. Many also make use of medications that help control their symptoms. Others may find relief in a healthy diet and a regular physical exercise regimen.

- *Anxiety Disorders* are the most frequently diagnosed mental disorders in the US. Most occur prior to adulthood. Symptoms include feelings of dread or apprehension and can extend to physical symptoms like a pounding or racing heart, sweating, headache or stomachache, or sleeplessness. Anxieties may be general or focused on circumstances or activities, such as certain social situations, phobias, or nonspecific situational discomfort that may result in panic attacks. While everyone experiences anxiety at times, an anxiety disorder is debilitating and often leads to social isolation, as a person avoids situations that provoke their individual fears.

- *Attention Deficit Hyperactivity Disorder (ADHD)* typically includes symptoms of inattention, hyperactivity, and impulsive behaviors. Some struggle with staying engaged in necessary activities long enough to complete them. Others struggle with attentiveness but not hyperactivity (ADD). ADHD can also be associated with other conditions, such as anxiety disorders or bipolar disorder, among others. Many individuals with ADHD find they can function well enough in their daily lives and forego medication. Others find medications help them focus or control impulsiveness.

- *Bipolar Disorder.* Once known as Manic Depression, Bipolar Disorder is characterized by mood swings that are more extreme than those experienced by most people. Diagnosis of Bipolar Disorder is dependent on the severity of the high and low moods and the duration of each. It may be misdiagnosed because it is often accompanied by delusions and/ or hallucinations. There are four subcategories of Bipolar Disorder, the two most common being Bipolar I Disorder and Bipolar II Disorder. Those with Bipolar I Disorder tend to experience longer periods of mania (more than 7 days) and may or may not experience depression. Those with Bipolar II Disorder experience depressive and manic episodes but with more frequent mood swings.

- *Borderline Personality Disorder* is characterized by extreme mood swings and inability to regulate behavior that can sometimes become dangerous; it is more commonly diagnosed in women. An emotional trigger often generates a prolonged and intense emotional response and leads to such symptoms as intense fear of abandonment, exaggerated avoidance of known triggers, depression, or feelings of unworthiness. Some patients attempt self-harm. Borderline

Personality Disorder is difficult to diagnose because many of the symptoms are similar to those of other disorders.

- *Delusional Disorder* appears along the Schizophrenia spectrum but may be less detrimental in everyday functioning than Schizophrenia, because the illness is limited to delusions and doesn't necessarily present other symptoms. There are degrees of impairment, depending on the extent of delusions. More detail about the effects of delusions may be found under "Schizophrenia."

- *Depression*, or in technical terms, Depressive Disorder, is more than simply feeling sad. Most of us feel sadness from time to time, but for someone with clinically diagnosed Depression, these feelings are extreme and sustained—for months, or sometimes years. NAMI estimates that 8.4% of US adults experienced a major depressive episode in 2020. During a depressive episode, an individual might experience loss of sleep or appetite, low energy or enthusiasm for once enjoyable activities, feelings of hopelessness, or suicidal ideation. To receive a diagnosis of Depressive Disorder, several of these symptoms must be present for more than two weeks.

- *Eating Disorders* are characterized by an obsessive focus on food and weight, such that normal functioning becomes difficult. They are more prevalent among women and tend to develop during adolescence or young adulthood. Eating disorders are a collection of conditions that include Anorexia Nervosa, Bulimia Nervosa, and Binge Eating Disorder. Each is defined by whether the food obsession causes eating too little, deliberate vomiting after eating, or eating too much in a short period of time. All of the conditions can be harmful to an individual's health, and in some cases, fatal. Eating disorders are often accompanied by anxiety, depression, or substance abuse.

• *Posttraumatic Stress Disorder (PTSD)* occurs when a trauma affects individuals so intensely that they are unable to function satisfactorily afterward. The trauma may be short-term, as in an accident or natural disaster event. Seemingly smaller traumas, sustained over a long period of time, may also result in PTSD. Military service in wartime is a well-known source of PTSD, but sustained childhood abuse or neglect and a long list of other stressors may cause the condition. Complex PTSD (C-PTSD) is complicated by challenges with emotion regulation and developing healthy relationships. PTSD is frequently associated with anxiety, substance use disorders, obsessive compulsive disorder, depression, and borderline personality disorder. Understanding of triggers and how to avoid or overcome being triggered by them is often effective treatment.

• *Schizoaffective Disorder* is commonly misdiagnosed, because symptoms of Schizophrenia such as delusions or hallucinations are present, in addition to symptoms of a mood disorder, such as mania or depression. Like those who struggle with the other disorders, a person with Schizoaffective Disorder is likely to exhibit disordered thinking. Treatments for Schizophrenia and Bipolar Disorder are often equally effective in treating Schizoaffective Disorder.

• *Schizophrenia* is the quintessential psychosis. Other mental diseases such as Delusional Disorder and Schizoaffective Disorder are also considered psychotic conditions, but only because of their presentation of positive Schizophrenia symptoms. Delusions, hallucinations, and disorganized thinking are primary indicators of Schizophrenia, but other negative symptoms like flat affect (negative or flat emotions) are also often present and may appear as Depressive Disorder. Many individuals with Schizophrenia suppress their positive symptoms, which makes early diagnosis difficult. Men tend to exhibit symptoms in their late teens, and women in their late twenties or early thirties. It is rare for symptoms to occur prior to age 12 or after age 40. Substance use disorders, Depressive Disorders, and PTSD or Obsessive Compulsive Disorder frequently accompany Schizophrenia. Suicidal thoughts or actions are not uncommon among individuals with Schizophrenia.

Recommended projects and discussions

1. Interview a family member of an individual with serious mental illness, using some of the questions listed in Appendix I and report on the family's efforts to advocate for their relative. What challenges do they face? How are these challenges a result of public policy?

2. Interview one or more first responders, such as an emergency medical technician, a firefighter, or law enforcement officer regarding how they were trained to deal with individuals experiencing a mental health crisis. Who conducted the training and how was it conducted? Did the first responder feel confident after the training in dealing with an individual with SMI? How could the training be improved to increase their confidence in such situations?

3. Research mental health legislation in your state. Describe one policy change you could advocate for that might benefit families dealing with mental illness. Create an advocacy action plan.

4. Visit or tour a community-based mental health program or clinic near you. Observe and assess its effectiveness and suggest revisions that would better serve their clients or patients.

5.   According to D. J. Jaffe, prison has replaced long-term psychiatric hospital commitment as a strategy for dealing with individuals who have an SMI. Do you agree or disagree? Compare and contrast these two scenarios as consequences of public policy and assess how well each serves its community. What might you suggest instead?

References

Aldridge, O. (2023). Integral Care, Austin's largest mental health care provider, approves 48 layoffs in next budget. *Austin Monitor* [Online] Available at: www.austinmonitor.com/stories/2023/09/integral-care-austins-largest-mental-health-care-provider-approves-48-layoffs-in-next-budget/ [Accessed 1 May 2025].

Amador, X., Flaum, M., Andreasen, N., Strauss, D., Yale, S., Clark, S., and Gorman, J. (1994). Awareness of illness in schizophrenia and schizoaffective and mood disorders. *Archives of General Psychiatry*. [Online] 51(10), pp. 826–836. Available at: https://pubmed.ncbi.nlm.nih.gov/7944872/ [Accessed 1 May 2025].

Batchelder, A. (2023). *Craving Spring: A mother's quest, a daughter's depression, and the Greek myth that brought them together.* Camanche, Iowa: Legacy Book Press.

Columbia Law School. (2017). Kimberlé Crenshaw on intersectionality, more than two decades later. [Online] Available at: www.law.columbia.edu/news/archive/kimberle-crenshaw-intersectionality-more-two-decades-later [Accessed 30 April 2025].

Dehbozorgi, R, et al. (2022). Barriers to family involvement in the care of patients with chronic mental illnesses: A qualitative study. [Online] *Frontiers in Psychiatry*, vol. 13. Available at: https://pmc.ncbi.nlm.nih.gov/articles/PMC9627781/ [Accessed 24 May 2025].

Dunn, J. (2002). Sibling relationships. In: P. K. Smith & C. H. Hart, eds., *Blackwell handbook of childhood social development*. Oxford, UK: Blackwell Publishing, (pp. 223–237).

EMDR Institute, Inc. (2025). What is EMDR Therapy?. [Online] Available at: www.emdr.com/what-is-emdr/ [Accessed 19 May 2025].

Fadlallah, R. et al. (2019) Using narratives to impact health policy-making: a systematic review. [Online] *Health Research Policy and Systems.* Available at: https://pmc.ncbi.nlm.nih.gov/articles/PMC 6402129/ [Accessed 25 June 2025].

Goodman, D, and Happell, B. (2006). The efficacy of family intervention in adolescent mental health. [Online] *The International Journal of Psychiatric Nursing Research.* Available at: https://pub med.ncbi.nlm.nih.gov/17016899/ [Accessed 24 May 2025].

Gray, K. (2022). Busting myths about people with mental illness and criminal activity. [Online] Association of Health Care Journalists. Available at: https://healthjournalism.org/blog/2022/ 01/busting-myths-about-people-with-mental-illness-and-crimi nal-activity/ [Accessed 30 April 2025].

Hahn, P. (2020). *The real myth of the schizophrenogenic mother.* [Online] Available at: www.madinamerica.com/2020/01/real-myth-schizophrenogenic-mother/ [Accessed 30 April 2025].

Hawkins, M. (2010). *How We Got Barb Back: The Story of My Sister's Reawakening After 30 Years of Schizophrenia.* Newburyport, MA: Red Wheel.

Hestmark, L. et al. (2023). Clinicians' perceptions of family involvement in the treatment of persons with psychotic disorders: a nested qualitative study. [Online] *Frontiers in Psychiatry.*14 Available at: https:// frontiersin.org/journals/psychiatry/articles/ 10.3389/fpsyt.2023.1175557/full [Accessed 24 May 2025].

Iannelli, V. (2024). *A history and timeline of autism.* [Online] Available at: www.verywellhealth.com/autism-timeline-2633213 [Accessed 30 April 2025].

Jaffe, D. J. (2017). *Insane Consequences: How the Mental Health Industry Fails the Mentally Ill.* New York City: Prometheus Books.

Mellifont, D. and Smith-Merry, J. (2021). *Disability, identity, and language choices: person-first, identity-first, and beyond.* [Blog]

Lived Places Publishing Blog. Available at: https://livedplacespub lishing.com/blog/disability-identity-and-language-choices-per son-first-identity-first-and-beyond/ [Accessed 30 April 2025].

Mokoena, A., Poggenpoel, M., Myburgh, C., and Temane, A. (2019). Lived experiences of couples in a relationship where one part- ner is diagnosed with a mental illness. *Curationis,* [Online] 42(1): 2015. Available at: https://pmc.ncbi.nlm.nih.gov/articles/PMC6779 990/#:~:text=In%20both%20studies%2C%20the%20couples,di- agnosed%20with%20a%20mental%20illness [Accessed 30 April 2025].

National Alliance on Mental Illness (n.d.). Mental health condi- tions. [Online] Available at: https://www.nami.org/about-mental- illness/mental-health-conditions/ [Accessed 23 June 2025].

National Alliance on Mental Illness (2021). *Texas State Fact Sheet.* [Online] Available at chrome-extension://efaidnbmnnnibpca- jpcglclefindmkaj/https://www.nami.org/wp-content/uploads/ 2023/07/TexasStateFactSheet.pdf [Accessed 23 June 2025].

Neuroscience News (2022). *New study maps the development of the 20 most common psychiatric disorders.* [Online] Available at: https://neurosciencenews.com/mental-health-disorder-diagnosis- 21960/ [Accessed 30 April 2025].

Ong, H., Fernandez, P., and Lim, H. (2021). Family engagement as part of managing patients with mental illness in primary care. *Singapore Medical Journal.* [Online] 62(5) pp. 213–219. Available at: https://pmc.ncbi.nlm.nih.gov/articles/PMC8801 858/ [Accessed 24 May 2025].

Pitschel-Walz, G., et.al. (2004). The effect of family interventions on relapse and rehospitalization in schizophrenia: a meta-analysis. *Psychiatry Online: Focus* [Online] Available at: https://psychiatr yonline.org/doi/full/10.1176/foc.2.1.78 [Accessed 24 May 2025].

Rasic, D., Hajek, T., Alda, M., and Uher, R. (2014). Risk of mental illness in offspring of parents with schizophrenia, bipolar dis- order, and major depressive disorder: A meta-analysis of family high-risk studies. *Schizophrenia Bulletin, 40*(1), 28–38. Available at: https://pubmed.ncbi.nlm.nih.gov/23960245/ [Accessed 30 April 2025].

Schiffman, J. et.al. (2015). Outcomes of a family peer education program for families of youth and adults with mental illness. *International Journal of Mental Health*, [Online] 44(4). Available at: https://pmc.ncbi.nlm.nih.gov/articles/PMC5548144/?utm [Accessed 24 May 2025].

Sher, L. and Kahn, R. (2019) Suicide in schizophrenia: An educational overview. *Medicina, 5*(7), p. 361. [Online] Available at: www.mdpi.com/1648-9144/55/7/361 [Accessed 1 May 2025].

Simpson, S. (2024) A look at the Texas mental health workforce shortage. *The Texas Tribune* [Online] July 17, 2024. Available at: https://www.texastribune.org/2024/07/17/texas-mental-health-workforce-explainer/ [Accessed 30 April 2025].

Suicide Prevention Center (2023). *Suicide and Serious Mental Illness*. [Online] Available at: https://sprc.org/about-suicide/scope-of-the-problem/suicide-and-serious-mental-illness/#:~:text=In%202021%2C%20individuals%20reporting%20past,2%25). [Accessed 1 May 2025].

US Dept. of Health and Human Services (2025). Summary of the HIPAA Privacy Rule. [Online] Available at: www.hhs.gov/hipaa/for-professionals/privacy/laws-regulations/index.html#:~:text=The%20Health%20Insurance%20Portability%20and%20Accountability%20Act%20of%201996%20(HIPAA,and%20security%20of%20health%20information [Accessed 25 June 2025].

Waldman, A. and Miller, M. (2024). What mental health care protections exist in your state? *ProPublica* [Online] August 29, 2024. Available at: https://governing.com/policy/what-mental-health-care-protections-exist-in-your-state [Accessed 24 May 2025].

Walker, N. (2014). *Neurodiversity: some basic terms and definitions.* [Blog] Neuroqueer. Available at: https://neuroqueer.com/neurodiversity-terms-and-definitions/ [Accessed 30 April 2025].

Yadav, G, McNamara, S. and Gunturu, S. (2024). Trauma-Informed Therapy. [Online] National Library of Medicine. Available at: www.ncbi.nlm.nih.gov/books/NBK604200/ [Accessed 19 May 2025].

Zhaori, G. (2020). Professor Robert Freedman and his contributions to psychiatric research. *Pediatric Investigation*. 4(2), 73–76. [Online] June 24, 2020. Available at: https://onlinelibrary.wiley.com/doi/10.1002/ped4.12201 [Accessed 6 June 2025].

Recommended further reading

1. *After Schizophrenia: The Story of My Sister's Reawakening After 30 Years of Schizophrenia* by Margaret Hawkins
2. *Craving Spring: A Mother's Quest, a Daughter's Depression, and the Greek Myth That Brought Them Together* by Ann Batchelder
3. *Hidden Valley Road: Inside the Mind of an American Family* by Robert Kolker
4. *Insane Consequences: How the Mental Health Industry Fails the Mentally Ill* by D. J. Jaffe
5. *The Center Cannot Hold: My Journey Through Madness* by Ellyn R. Saks

About the author

Janice Airhart has been a medical technologist, biomedical research tech, freelance writer and editor, science teacher to pregnant teens, bioscience program representative, and adjunct English professor. Her memoir, *Mother of My Invention: A Motherless Daughter Memoir* was published in 2022. Her essays and articles have appeared in *The Sun*, *The Science Teacher*, *Lutheran Woman Today*, *Concho River Review*, Story Circle Network's *Real Women Write* 2021 and 2023 anthologies, among other publications. Her experiences teaching science to pregnant and parenting teen girls are described in *What Teaching Teen Moms Taught Me: Lessons from a High School Classroom*, published by Lived Places Publishing in 2025. Airhart is also the author of a Substack newsletter, "Subject to Change".

Index